Spurgeon's Sermons on
New Testament Miracles

Charles Haddon Spurgeon

Grand Rapids, MI 49501

Spurgeon's Sermons on New Testament Miracles
by Charles H. Spurgeon.

Copyright © 1995 by Kregel Publications.

Published by Kregel Publications, a division of Kregel, Inc., P.O. Box 2607, Grand Rapids, MI 49501. Kregel Publications provides trusted, biblical publications for Christian growth and service. Your comments and suggestions are valued.

All rights reserved. No part of this book may be reproduced, stored in a retrieval system, or transmitted in any form or by any means—electronic, mechanical, photocopy, recording, or otherwise—without written permission of the publisher, except for brief quotations in printed reviews.

Cover artwork: Don Ellens
Cover and book design: Alan G. Hartman

Library of Congress Cataloging-in-Publication Data

Spurgeon, C. H. (Charles Haddon), 1834–1892.
  [Sermons on New Testament miracles]
  Spurgeon's Sermons on New Testament Miracles / by Charles H. Spurgeon.
    p.   cm.—(C.H. Spurgeon sermon series)
    1. Miracles—Sermons. 2. Bible. N.T.—Sermons.
3. Sermons, English. I. Title. II. Series: Spurgeon, C. H. (Charles Haddon), 1834–1892. C. H. Spurgeon sermon series.
BS2545.M5S68 1995   226.7'06—dc20   95-8340
                                                               CIP

ISBN 0-8254-3784-9 (pbk.)

        1 2 3 4 5 printing / year 99 98 97 96 95

Printed in the United States of America

Contents

1. The Cripple at Lystra (Acts 14:9–10) 5
2. Aeneas (Acts 9:32–35) 18
3. Nothing but Leaves (Mark 11:13) 32
4. The Waterpots at Cana (John 2:7) 46
5. An Astounding Miracle (Mark 1:21–28) 60
6. Impotence and Omnipotence (John 5:5–9) 74
7. Carried by Four (Luke 5:16–26) 85
8. The Free Agency of Christ (Mark 8:22–25) 99
9. The Two Draughts of Fishes (Luke 5:4; John 21:6) 110
10. Good Cheer from Grace Received (Matt. 9:20–22; Luke 8:42–48) 124
11. A Sabbath Miracle (Luke 13:10–13) 138
12. Young Man, Is This for You? (Luke 7:11–17) 148

1
The Cripple at Lystra

The same heard Paul speak: who stedfastly beholding him, and perceiving that he had faith to be healed, said with a loud voice, Stand upright on thy feet. And he leaped and walked (Acts 14:9–10).

I have read in your hearing the story of the preaching of Paul and Barnabas in the town of Lystra. The name of Christ was there totally unknown. They were a sort of country people, partly pastoral and partly agricultural, who seem to have been deeply sunken in superstition. At the gates of their city there stood a great temple dedicated to Jupiter, and they appear to have been his zealous votary. Coming down from the mountainside, Paul and Barnabas enter the town, and when a fitting time has come, they stand up in the marketplace, or the street, and begin to talk concerning Jesus, the Son of God, who had come down from heaven, had suffered and died, and had again ascended up on high. The people gather around them. Among the rest a cripple listens with very marked attention. They preach again. The crowds are still greater, and on one occasion, while Paul is in the middle of a sermon, using his eyes to watch the audience as all preachers should do, and not looking up at the ceiling or at the gallery-front as some preachers are wont to do, he marks this cripple, fixes his eyes upon him, and looks earnestly in his face. Either by the exercise of his judgment or by the promptings of revelation, the apostle gathers that this man has faith—faith to be healed. In order to attract the attention of the people, to glorify the name of Christ, to publish more widely His glorious fame, and to make the miracle well known, Paul stops the sermon and with a loud voice cries, "Stand upright on thy feet!" The cripple leaps and praises God. The population are all amazed, and knowing that there was a tradition that Jupiter and Mercury had once appeared in that very town,

---

This sermon was taken from *The Metropolitan Tabernacle Pulpit* and was preached at the Metropolitan Tabernacle, Newington, in 1864.

a tradition preserved in the *Metamorphoses* of Ovid to the present day, they at once conclude that surely Jupiter and Mercury must be come again.

They fix upon Barnabas, who was probably the elder and the nobler-looking man for Jupiter; and as Jupiter was always attended by Mercurius, as a messenger, and Mercury was the god of eloquence, they conclude that Paul must be Mercury. They rush to the temple; they tell the priests that the gods have come down. The priests, only too ready to foster popular credulity and pander to it, bring forth the sacred bullocks and the garlands and are about to offer sacrifice before Paul and Barnabas. Such homage these men of God indignantly refuse. They rend their clothes; they beseech them to do no such thing for they are nothing but men. Yet hardly with earnest words can they stay the people. But the next day certain Jews came thither and produce a counter irritation in the simple minds of the people. No very difficult task where a rude fanaticism rouses the wild passions of the mob. Such an assembly must rage, whether it be with redundant applause or with derisive jeers. Accordingly, Paul finds himself exposed to peril; he is stoned through the streets, dragged forth as dead, and left by the very men who worshiped him but yesterday as a god, left to die as a villain outside the city gates. But Paul's preaching had not been in vain. There were some few disciples who remained faithful. His ministry was rewarded and owned of God.

There are two or three points in this narrative to which I shall call your attention tonight, making, however, the lame man the center of the picture. We shall notice, first of all, *what preceded this lame man's faith*; secondly, *wherein lay his faith to be healed*; and thirdly, *what is the teaching of the miracle itself, and the blessing which the lame man obtained through faith*.

What Preceded His Faith?

That "faith cometh by hearing, and hearing by the word of God," is a great and universal rule; but the hearing of what? Doubtless the hearing of the Gospel is intended. On turning to your Bibles you will find it is written—"And there they preached the gospel." What, Paul, do you not change your voice? You have preached the Gospel in the cities of Iconium and Antioch, where there were enlightened and intelligent hearers; if the Gospel suited them, surely it will not do for these wolfish boors! Why go and preach to these poor, ignorant, superstitious fanatics the very same truths which you spoke to your enlightened Jewish brethren? But he does do so, my friends. The very Gospel which he preached at Damascus in the synagogue he preaches here at Lystra in the marketplace. He makes no difference between the education of his

The Cripple at Lystra

hearers in different places; he has the same Gospel to preach to them both.

You recollect that Paul went to Ephesus, and Ephesus, as a city, was besotted with a belief in sorcery. The people had given themselves up to practice magical arts. What is the right way to begin to preach at Ephesus? Deliver a course of lectures upon the impossibility and absurdity of such superstition? No, sir, nothing of the kind. Preach Christ, preach the Gospel; and as Jesus Christ is lifted up they bring their magical books and make a bonfire of them in the open forum. But here is a polished governor, Sergius Paulus, sitting upon the judgment seat. What shall be preached to him? Would it not be well to begin with a dissertation on politics, and to show that the Christian religion does not interfere with proper government, that it does not stir up the people to anarchy? No, sir, nothing of the kind. There is nothing for Sergius Paulus any more than there is for Elymas the sorcerer but the preaching of the Gospel of Jesus Christ. Paul goes to Athens. Now the Athenians are one of the most learned and philosophical of the whole race of humanity. What will Paul preach there? The Gospel, the whole Gospel, and nothing but the Gospel. He may change his *tones*, but never his *matter*. It is the same remedy for the same disease, be the people what they may. He comes to Corinth, and here you have not only polished manners, but the very refinement of vice. It is a city, an emporium of trade, and a sort of central depot of sin. What then? Will he now, to please the trader, assume a different dialect? Not he! The Christ for Athens is the Christ for Corinth too.

And now see him. He has come to Lycaonia and is preaching at Lystra. Here is an ignorant set of people who worship an image. Why does he not begin by preaching of the deity? Why does he not talk to them of the Trinity in unity? Why does he not try and confute their notions about their gods? No, my dear sir, he will do nothing of the kind; that may be done incidentally, but the first and the last thing that Paul will do at Lystra is there he will preach the Gospel. O glorious Gospel of the blessed God! Wherever we take you, you are suited to the wants of people. Take you to Persia with all its gems and jewels, and you do suit the monarch on his throne; or take you to the naked savage with all his poverty and squalid filth, and you do suit him too. You may be preached, thrice glorious wisdom of God, to the wisest of humanity; but you are not too great a mystery to be understood and believed even by the fools and the babes. The things that are not can receive you as well as the things that are. Never, I pray you brethren, lose heart in the power of the Gospel. Do not believe that there exists any one, much less any race of people, for whom the Gospel is not fitted. Wherever you go, do not cut, and trim, and shape, and alter; but just bring out the whole truth as God has taught it to you, and rest assured that you will be to God a sweet savor of Christ in every place, both in them who are saved and in them who perish.

What then, was this Gospel which the apostle Paul did preach everywhere? Well, it was a Gospel which had in it three things, *certain facts, certain doctrines*, and *certain commands*.

It was a *Gospel of facts*. Every time Paul stood up to preach he told the following unvarnished tale: God, looking upon humanity, beheld them lost and ruined. Out of love to them He sent His only begotten Son, the Lord Jesus Christ, who was born of the Virgin Mary, lived some thirty-two or thirty-three years a life of spotless innocence and perfect obedience to God. He was God; He was man. In due time He was delivered up by the traitor Judas. He was crucified, and actually put to death. Though He was the Lord of life and glory, who only has immortality, yet He bowed His head and gave up the ghost. After three days He rose again, and showed Himself to many of His disciples, so that they were well assured He was the same person who had been put into the grave. When the forty days were finished He ascended up to heaven in the sight of them all, where He sits at the right hand of God, and shall also come before long a second time to judge both the living and the dead. These were the facts which Paul would state. God was made flesh and dwelt among us, and we beheld His glory, the glory as of the only begotten of the Father, full of grace and truth. "This is a faithful saying, and worthy of all acceptation, that Christ Jesus came into the world to save sinners; of whom I am chief." Briefly, these were the facts which Paul would preach, and if any one of these facts be preached doubtfully, or be left out of any ministry, then the Gospel is not preached; for the foundations upon which the Gospel rests have been removed, and then what can the righteous do?

Following upon these facts, Paul preached *certain doctrines*, the doctrines flowing out of the facts. To wit, he preached that Jesus Christ had offered a full atonement to divine wrath for the sin of His people, so that whosoever would believe on Him, and trust Him, should be saved. The doctrine of the Atonement would form the most prominent feature in the Gospel of the apostle Paul. Christ also has suffered for us, the just for the unjust, to bring us to God. "God commendeth his love toward us, in that, while we were yet sinners, Christ died for the ungodly." Then would come the doctrine of pardon. Paul with glowing tongue would tell how God could be just, and yet the justifier of those who believe; how all manner of sin and iniquity shall be forgiven to people, the simple condition being that the person believes in Christ, and this not so much the person's own work as a gift of the Holy Spirit. Everywhere Paul would be unmistakable in this—Ye chief of sinners, look to the wounds of Jesus, and your sins shall be forgiven you.

Equally clear would he be upon the doctrine of justification. "Christ," he would say, "will wash you; nay, more, He will clothe you; the perfect holiness of His character shall be imputed to you, and being justified, you shall have peace with God, and there shall be no condemnation, because you are in Christ Jesus." I think I see the flashing eye of the apostle; I think I listen to his earnest voice, while he pleads with people to lay hold upon eternal life, to look to Jesus Christ, to forsake the deeds of the law, to put their trust in nothing which comes from humanity, but to look to Jesus, and to Jesus only. These great truths—atonement, pardon, and justification—with all the other truths connected with them, of which we cannot now speak particularly, were just the Gospel which the apostle Paul preached.

And out of these we said there sprung *certain commands*. The commands were these—"Believe on the Lord Jesus Christ, and thou shalt be saved." Nor do I suppose that the apostle for a moment stammered to preach that other command—"Arise, and be baptized." He would not preach half the Gospel, but the whole of it—"He that believeth and is baptized shall be saved; but he that believeth not shall be damned"; and often after his hearers had cried, "What must we do to be saved," and they had believed in Christ, they would say to him—"See, here is water, what doth hinder me to be baptized?"

The apostle then preached a Gospel which was made up of certain authenticated facts, out of which there flowed certain most gracious evangelical doctrines, which were enforced and driven home with divine authority by Christ's own commands. "Well," says one, "do you think the world will be turned upside down by this?" Sirs, it has been, and it will be again. In vain do those who seek after human learning, and who aim at dreamy sentiment or spurious science in preference to the standard teaching which is from above, attempt to find a nobler instrument. This is the great battering ram which shall yet shake the bastions of error. This is the sword, the true Excalibur, which, if any one knows how to wield it, shall cut through joints and marrow, and make him more than a conqueror. He or she who gets a hold of the Gospel of Christ, and knows how to use it, has that before which the devils tremble, and in the presence of which angels adore, which cherubs long to look into, and which God Himself smiles upon as His noblest work. The truth we proclaim is not that which is discovered by us, but that which has been delivered to us. Do you ask, then, where this man's faith came from? It came from Paul's preaching of the Gospel.

In What Lay This Man's Faith?

Paul looked at the man, we are told, and perceived *"that he had faith to be healed."* What does this "faith to be healed" mean? In this man's case I think it was something like this. Poor fellow! As he listened to Paul's preaching, he thought perhaps—"Well, that looks like true; that seems to be the truth. It is the truth. I am sure it is true. If it is true that Jesus Christ is so great a Savior, perhaps I may be healed. These lame legs of mine, which never would carry me anywhere, may yet come straight. I—I—I think they may. I hope they may. I believe they may. I know it can be done if Christ wills it. I believe that, and from what Paul says of Christ's character, I think He must be willing to do it. I will ask the apostle. The first convenient season that I have I will lift up my cry, for I believe it can be done, and I think there is a perfect willingness, both in the mind of the apostle and of the Master that it should be done. I believe it will be done, and that I shall yet stand upright." Then Paul said to him, "Stand upright on thy feet," and he did so in a moment, for "he had faith to be healed."

Do you think I am overstraining the probabilities of the case? You will perhaps say, "It does not appear that Paul had any communication with the poor cripple before the miracle was performed." Now I venture to draw quite an opposite inference. I know from my own experience that it is no uncommon thing for one individual to arrest the preacher's attention. The group of countenances which lay before him in a large assembly like the present might to the first glance of a stranger look confused and inexplicable, as a Chinese grammar does to those who know not the language. But you need not doubt that a practiced eye can learn to read the one as well as the other. The languor and indifference of some; the curious inquiring look of others; the cold, critical attention of a considerable number; and the countenances of those who are rather absorbed in a train of thought just awakened in their own minds—these have all a peculiar impressiveness, and form a picture which often reacts upon us, and kindles a vehement desire in our breasts to reach the souls of those who, for a brief hour, hang upon our words. But there will sometimes be one who has faith dazzling in his very eyes, as they are fixed with an intentness of which it were vain for me to attempt a description, seeming to drink in every word and every syllable of a word, until the preacher becomes as absorbed in that person as the person had been in the preacher. And while he pursues the discourse, gaining liberty at every step, until he forgets the formality of the pulpit in the freedom of conversation with the people, he perceives that at last this person has heard the very truth which meets his case. There is no concealing it. His features have suddenly relaxed. He listens still, but it is no longer with painful anxiety; a calm satisfaction is palpable on his face now. That soul of communion which is in the eye has unraveled the secret. Preacher and hearer, unknown to all the rest of the audience, have secretly saluted each other, and met on the common

The Cripple at Lystra

ground of a vital faith. The anxious one feels that it can be done. And I can readily conclude that the apostle perceived that feeling with greater certainty than he would have done had the man whispered it in his ears. So have I sometimes known that the exhortation to believe has become from these lips a positive command to the struggling conscience of someone who has been brought to a point where the remedy is instantly applied, and the cure instantly effected.

Most unquestionably there is such a thing as faith to be saved. I do not know how many here may possess it; but, thank God, there are hundreds of you here who have faith that *you are* saved. That is better; that is the ripest faith, the faith which knows you are saved and rejoices in hope of the glory of God. Alas! there are others who have no faith at all. But it is with those who have faith, and that only faith *to be* saved, not faith that *you are* saved, I am more particularly concerned at this moment.

Shall I describe this faith to be saved? For I believe that there may be some here who may just now stand upright on their feet, some who may at this time leap for joy of heart because they are saved and did not know it. You have faith, but you have not fully exercised it. Now, you believe that Jesus Christ is God's Son? "Yes." That He has made a full atonement for His people? "Yes." You believe that they are His people who trust Him? "Yes." You believe He is worthy to be trusted? "Yes." You have nothing else to trust to? "No, sir." You depend on nothing which you have ever felt, or thought, or done? "No, sir, I depend on nothing but Christ." And you do, after a sort of fashion, trust Christ. You hope that one of these days He will save you, and you think, and sometimes you almost know He will. You are ready to trust Him. You do believe He is able, you do not think He is unwilling; you have got faith in His ability, and you have almost got faith in His willingness; sometimes you half think to yourself, "I am a child of God." But then, there is some ugly "but" comes in. Those lame legs again; those lame legs again. You are still afraid. You have faith to be saved, but you have not the full assurance of faith which can utter forth this joyous psalm, "Behold, God is my salvation; I will trust, and not be afraid: for the Lord Jehovah is my strength and my song; he also is become my salvation."

Well now, I do not know whether I have picked you out, whether I have given a right description of you or not. I recollect the time when I was in that state. I can honestly say I did not doubt Christ. I three parts believed that He would save me. I knew He was worthy of my trust, and I did trust Him as far as this, that I resolved if I did perish, I would perish crying to Him, and that if I was cast away, it should be clinging to the cross. I believe I had faith to be saved, and was for months in bondage when there was no necessity that I should have been in bondage at all, for, when there is faith to be saved, then the man only needs that gracious command—"Stand upright on thy feet," and forthwith he leaps out of his infirmity, and walks freely in the integrity of his heart.

The Spiritual Teaching of the Miracle, and of the Blessing Conferred

Are there not many, who though they have faith to be saved, are still entirely lame or painfully limping? The reasons may be different in different cases. Some have been so stunned by the grief which they have suffered on account of sin, and the frightful convictions through which they have passed that while they do believe that Christ is able and willing to save, they cannot get a hold of the fact that they are saved. Such is the faintness of spirit and the languishing of soul brought on by long despair. "Stand upright on thy feet," you trembling sinner. If you believe in Jesus, whatever your fears may be there is no cause for them. As for your sins, they were laid on Him, every one of them, and though you have been sore broken in the land of dragons, thus says the Lord to you, "I have put away thy sin; thou shalt not die; I have blotted out like a cloud thy transgressions, and like a thick cloud thy sins." Rejoice, then, and be glad. If you do trust Christ, you are saved; though as yet it only looks like faith which heralds the tidings of a salvation which has not yet arrived. Still, it is the grace of God which brings salvation which has enabled you to believe; and he who believes on the Son has everlasting life. O receive the welcome message; spring up at the sound of the words; stand upright on your feet and rejoice.

Some are still lame *through ignorance* though they have faith. They do not know what being saved is. They entertain wrong expectations. They are trusting in Christ, but they do not feel any surprising emotions. They have not had any remarkable dreams, or visions, or striking ablutions of excited joy, and therefore, though they have faith to be saved, they have not the faith of a present salvation. They are waiting for something, they hardly know what, to embellish their faith, or to fortify it with signs and wonders. Now, poor soul, wherefore do you wait? These things are not necessary to salvation. In fact, the fewer you have of them, I think, the better, especially of things which are visionary. I rather tremble for those who talk much about sensible evidences; they are too often the frivolities of unstable hearts. Beloved, though you may have never had any ecstatic joys, or suffered any deep depression of your spirits, if you are resting on Christ, it does not matter one whit what your feelings have been or have not been. Do you expect to have an electric shock, or to go through some mysterious operation? The operation is mysterious, too mysterious for you to discern it; but all that you have to do with is this—"Do I believe in Jesus? Am I simply

The Cripple at Lystra 13

depending upon Him for everything?" If you do, you are saved; and I pray you to believe this. Stand upright on your feet, and leap for joy. For whether you believe it or not, if you are now depending upon Christ, your sins are forgiven you; you are a child of God; you are an heir of heaven.

How many, too, are kept lame because of *a fear of self-deception.* "I do trust Christ, but I am afraid lest I should deceive myself. Suppose I were to get confidence, and it should be presumption! Suppose I should think myself saved, and I am not!" Now, if you were dealing with yourself, there would be reason to be afraid of presumption; but your faith has to deal with God, who cannot deceive you, and with Christ who will never tempt you to be a deceiver. Does not the Lord Jesus Christ Himself tell you that if you believe in Him you are saved? You believe that, do you not? Then, soul, if you believe on Him, it is not presumption to say, "I am saved." Away with all that affectation of modesty, which some good people think to be so pretty—saying, "I hope"; "I trust"; but "I feel such doubts, such fears, and such gloomy misgivings." My dear sir, that is not humility; that is a vain unseemly questioning of God. The God and Father of our Lord Jesus Christ tells you, and He gives His own unequivocal word for it, that if you rest upon Christ you rest upon a rock; that if you believe in Him you are not condemned. Is it an evidence of the lowliness of your heart that you suspect the veracity of God or the faithfulness of His promise? Surely this were no fruit of the meekness of wisdom. No, beloved; it may seem too good to be true, but it is not too good for my God to give, though it is too good for you to receive. You have His word for it that if you trust His Son to save you, and simply trust Him, and Him alone, even if the pillars of the heavens should shake, yet you would be saved. If the foundations of the earth should reel, and the whole earth should like a vision pass away, yet this eternal promise and oath of God must stand fast.

Others again cannot stand upright on their feet because they are afraid that *if they did begin they would go back again, and so bring dishonor to Christ.* This would be a very proper fear if you had anything to do with keeping yourselves. If you had to carry yourselves to heaven it would be reasonable enough for you to despair of doing it. Of your own impotence it is impossible you can be too deeply convinced. You cannot do anything whatever, but Christ gives you His promise to preserve you even to the end. If you believe on Him you shall be saved. He does not say you shall be saved for a year, or for twenty years, and then, perhaps, be lost at last. No; but "he that believeth and is baptized, shall be saved." If one person who believes in Christ is cast away, that promise of Christ is not true. Friends, it is true, and it must be true, and let its glorious truth be sweetly familiar with you now—if you give your soul to Christ, putting simple faith in His person as the Son of God, and in His work as the Mediator between God and man, you shall as surely see His face within the pearly gates of heaven as your eyes see me tonight. There may be a question about your seeing me, but there can be no question about Christ fulfilling His promise and keeping His word. Now sit down in the dust no longer, you doubting, mourning, trembling sinner. With a loud voice I say to you, as Paul did, "Stand upright on thy feet." Wherefore do you mourn? There is nothing to mourn about. Your sin is forgiven; your eternal salvation is secure; a crown in heaven is provided for you, and a harp of gold awaits you. If you believe in Jesus none can lay anything to your charge. Not even the principalities of darkness shall be able to prevail against you. Eternal love secures you against the malice of hell. Stand upright, then, on your feet, for if you believe you are saved, completely saved, saved in time, and for eternal days, saved in the Lord with an everlasting salvation.

Then possibly there is one here who cannot stand upright *because of his many sins*. Ah! while I have been talking about Christ it may be something has been saying in your heart, "Ah! ah! what is it? Christ taking people's sins, suffering in their stead? That suits me. Is God doing this? Ah! then He must be able to save, and I am told that whosoever trusts in Him shall never perish; is it so? Why, here I am; I who have not been in a place of worship for months, for years, I have strayed in here tonight, and if what this man says be true, well then I will even venture my soul upon it. I have got nothing, I know, but he says there is nothing wanted. I am not prepared to trust Christ, but he says there is no preparation required, and if I trust Jesus Christ just as I am, Christ will save me. Why, I will do it; by the grace of God I will do it; can He save me?" Then comes in the bitter reflection—"Look what a sinner I have been! Why, I would be ashamed to say how foully I have sinned; God must shut me out. I have been too great a villain, too gross an offender. I have cursed and sworn at such a rate; he cannot mean that if I trust Christ I shall be saved. I believe He can save me. I see the fitness of the plan, and the excellency of it. I believe it, but see what a sinner I am!" Sinner, stand upright on your feet, for "all manner of sin and blasphemy shall be forgiven unto men." Return, wanderer, return to your Father's house! He comes to meet you. On your neck He will fall, and you shall be His child forever. Only believe in His Son Jesus Christ, and though this be the first time you have ever heard His Word, I would settle my eyes upon you earnestly, and say, "Stand upright on thy feet."

Oh! how often I do wish that somebody had come to me when I was under depression of mind, and had told me about the simple Gospel of Jesus Christ. I think I would have stood upright on my feet long before I did, but, alas! I kept hearing about what people felt before they believed in Christ—very proper preaching—and I was afraid I did not feel it, though now I know I did. I heard a great deal about what Christians ought to be, and a great deal more about God's elect, what they are in His esteem, but I did not know whether I was one of God's elect, and I knew I was not what I ought to be. Oh, for the trumpet of the archangel to sound the words, "*Believe and live*," as loud as the voice which shall wake the dead in their graves! and Oh, for the quickening Spirit to go with voice, as it shall go with the ringing of the archangel's trump, when the graves shall open, and the dead shall arise! Go, you who know it, and tell it everywhere, for there are multitudes, I doubt not, who are really seeking Christ, and who have His Spirit in them, but it is as the prophet has it, "The children have come to the birth and there is no strength to bring forth." They have come to the very edge of light, and they only want one helping hand to bring them into noonday. They are slipping about in the Slough of Despond, and they are almost out of it, but they want just a helping hand to pull them out. This hand of help is stretched out by thus telling them, telling them plainly, it is in Jesus their help is found, and that trusting Him, relying upon Him, they shall never perish, neither shall any pluck them out of His hand.

I would to God that some of you who have been long hearing me might be found in this class. I have been bowed down in spirit at some sad things which have been brought to my hearing of late. I know that there are some here, and there always have been some few attending my ministry, who have a personal affection for me, and who listen to the Word with very great attention, and who, moreover, are very greatly moved by it, but who have some besetting sin which they either cannot or will not give up. They do renounce it for a time, but either bad associates, or else the strength of their passions take them away again. Oh, sirs! I wish you would take warning. There was one of whom we had some sort of hope who listened to our ministry. There came a turning point with him; it was this, either that he must give up sin, or else give up coming to the Tabernacle; and what—oh! what became of him? I could indicate the place where he sat. *He died of delirium tremens!* And I do not wonder. When you have heard the Gospel preached Sabbath after Sabbath, when your response to the solemn appeals you have earnestly listened to has only been that you reject Christ and refuse eternal life—is it any marvel that in making the choice of your own damnation reason should resign its seat as director of your actions, and cease to curb your headstrong will, leaving the maddened passions to dash on with reckless fury, and precipitate your destruction.

Am I clear of their blood? I have asked myself the question. I may not be in some things, but I know I am as far as my ministry is concerned. I have not shunned to declare to any of you the whole counsel of God. When I have known any vice, or any folly—which of you have I been afraid of, or before whom of you all have I trembled? God is my witness; Him have I served in the spirit; if these turn aside to their crooked ways, they have not done it without well knowing the consequences. No, they have not done it without being warned and entreated, and persuaded to look to Jesus Christ. And I do conjure some of you—you know to whom I refer—I do conjure those of you who have a conscience which is not seared, but who, nevertheless, persevere in your sins—I conjure you by the love of God, do me this one favor at the last: if you choose your own ruin, bear witness for me that I have not hesitated to warn you of it. I had infinitely rather, however, that you would do yourselves this great favor, to love your own souls. If you have anything to throw into the fire, throw it in, but let it not be your soul. If you have anything to lose, go and lose it, but do not lose your soul. Sirs, if you must play the fool, indulge your sport at a cheaper rate than this. If sin be worth having, then I pray you pay a cheaper price than your own souls for it, for it does seem to me so pitiful, so sorrowful a thing, that you who have been so short a time among us and are passing away before my very eyes should still prefer the fleeting joy of the moment to the eternal joy, and risk everlasting torment for temporary mirth. By the tears of Jesus when He wept over Jerusalem, by the blood of Jesus which He shed for guilty human beings, by the heart of the eternal Father who wills not the death of a sinner but had rather that he should turn to Him and live, I pray you be wise and consider your ways. Choose you this day whom you will serve, and may the Lord guide your choice. May you fall into the arms of divine mercy and say, "If You will help me, Jesus, here I am; I give myself to You."

May my Master teach me how to address you if I do not know how to gasp the words of simplicity, tenderness, of terrible apprehension, but of persuasive power. If there were any words in any language that would melt you, this tongue is at your service to utter them. If there is any form of speech, though it should make me to be called vulgar and subject me to the shame and hissing which once I endured, if the furnace could be heated seven times hotter than that, I would but laugh at it if I might but win your souls. Tell me, sirs, how shall I put the case? Would you have argument? I wish that I could reason with you. Would you have tears? There, let them flow! You dry eyes, why do you not weep more for these perishing souls? Would you have God's Word without my word? Sirs, I would read it, and let my tongue be dumb if that would teach you. Would my death save you? That God who sees in secret knows that tonight it were a joy to me to enter into my rest, and so it were little for me to talk of being willing to give a life for you, and

The Cripple at Lystra

it were, indeed, but a trifle to me. Oh! why will you perish? Why should I plead with you, and you not care for yourselves? What is it that besets you? Poor moths! Are you dazzled with the flames? Are you not content to have singed your wings? Must they also consume body and soul? How can you make your bed in hell? How can you abide with eternal burnings? In the name of Jesus of Nazareth, I command you—for I can do no less—I command you to turn to Him and live. Believe on Him and you shall be saved. But remember, at your hazard you reject the message tonight. It may be the last message that shall ever come to your soul with power, if you cast this away—

> What chains of vengeance must they feel,
> Who slight the bonds of love?

I would have you saved just now. I cannot talk about tomorrow. I would have you decide it at once. Oh! you have come as far as this twenty times, and have you gone back again? You have been aroused, you have made vows and you have broken them, resolutions and you have belied them. O sirs, for God's sake do not lie to the Almighty again. Now be true this time. May the Spirit of God make you speak the truth, even though you should be compelled to say through your wickedness, "I will not submit myself to the Son of God." Do speak the truth. Procrastinate not. As Elijah said, "How long halt ye between two opinions?" so say I. If God be God serve Him, but if Baal be God serve him. But do not keep on coming here and then going to the tavern. Do not come and take your seat here and then go to the brothel. Sirs, do not this foul scandal for God's sake, and for your own sake. If you will serve the Devil serve him and be a true servant to him. If you mean to go to hell, go there; but if you seek eternal life and joys to come, give up these things. Renounce them. Why drink poison and drink medicine too? Have done with one or the other and be honest. Be honest to your own souls. May the Lord grant that tonight some may have given to them, not only faith to be saved, but the faith which saves, for His name's sake. Amen.

2
Aeneas

And it came to pass, as Peter passed throughout all quarters, he came down also to the saints which dwelt at Lydda. And there he found a certain man named Aeneas, which had kept his bed eight years, and was sick of the palsy. And Peter said unto him, Aeneas, Jesus Christ maketh thee whole: arise, and make thy bed. And he arose immediately. And all that dwelt in Lydda and Saron saw him, and turned to the Lord (Acts 9:32–35).

I may not hope that I shall see you all again, and so, as I have the opportunity of only preaching one sermon to you, I must make it as full as I can of *essence of Gospel*, from beginning to end. We have heard of a chaplain who preached in a jail, who selected a subject which he divided into two heads. The first part was the sinner's disease. This he took for his topic on one Sabbath, and closed the sermon by saying that he should preach upon the sinner's remedy upon the following Sunday. Now, there were several of the prisoners hanged on the Monday, according to the custom of the bad old times, so that they did not hear that part of the discourse which it was most necessary for them to hear. It would have been well to have told out the great news of salvation at once to men so near their end, and I think that in every sermon, if the preacher confines himself to one subject, and leaves out essential Gospel truth under the notion that he will preach salvation by Jesus another day, he is very unwise, for some of his congregation may be dead and gone—alas, some of them lost—before he will have the opportunity of coming to the grand and all-important point, namely, the way of salvation. We will not fall into that evil tonight. We will try to shoot at the very center of our target, and preach the plan of salvation as completely as we can; and may

---

This sermon was taken from *The Metropolitan Tabernacle Pulpit* and was preached on Sunday evening, July 16, 1876.

Aeneas

God grant that His blessing may rest on it, the Holy Spirit working with it.

I shall only preach this one sermon to some of you. You will, therefore, have the greater patience with me, as I shall not inflict myself upon you again. But, if we are to have only one communication with each other, let us come to real practical business and waste no time tonight. A good deal of sermon hearing is mere trifling; let us come to matter-of-fact preaching and hearing at this time. I am afraid that some sermon preaching is playing too—fine words and oratorical fireworks, but no agony for souls. We mean business tonight. My heart will not be satisfied unless many of you who came in here without Christ shall go down those steps saved by His atoning blood. Bitter will be my disappointment if many do not lay hold of Jesus, and realize in their own souls Peter's words, "Jesus Christ maketh thee whole." I have faith in the Great Physician that many of you will go away whole tonight though sin-sick when you came into this house of prayer. Much supplication has gone up to heaven for this, and the Lord hears prayer; therefore do I reckon that miracles of healing will surely be wrought in this house on this occasion.

To the point, then. Peter came to Lydda and found one who bore the name of Aeneas. No mighty warrior, however, but a poor paralyzed man who had been confined to his bed for eight long years. Touched with a sight of the man's feebleness, Peter felt the impulse of the Spirit upon him; looking at him as he lay there, he said, "Aeneas, Jesus Christ maketh thee whole: arise, and make thy bed." Touched by the same Spirit who inspired the apostle, the man believed the message—believed that Christ had healed him, at once rose and made his bed, and in an instant was perfectly restored. Now let us hear something about this man. We are not to hear Virgil sing, "arms and the man," but we are to let Luke tell us of the man and his Savior.

He Was Truly Sick

In the first place, then, it is very clear that the man was truly sick. Had he not been *really sick*, the incident before us would have been all a piece of imposture—a feint and a pretense from beginning to end. But he was hopelessly infirm. He had been anxiously watched by his friends for eight years, and was so completely palsied that during all those years he had not left his bed, which had grown hard as a stone beneath him. Now, as there is no room for a great cure unless there is a great sickness, so there is no room for God's great grace unless there is great sin. Jesus Christ did not come into the world to save sham sinners, but real sinners. Neither did He descend from heaven to seek those who are not diseased with sin, for the whole have no need of a physician, but He has come to seek those who are deeply diseased and to give them real healing. This man's sickness was no imaginary ill, for he could not move; his hands and feet were quite paralyzed. If in any limb there was a measure of motion, it was only a tremulous quiver, which rather indicated growing weakness than remaining force. He was bereaved of all strength. Are you such by nature, my friend, in a spiritual sense? Certainly you are so; but have you found it out? Has the Spirit of God made you feel that you can do nothing right apart from Him, and that you are altogether ruined and palsied unless Jesus Christ can save you? If so, do not despair because you feel how terribly your soul is smitten; on the contrary, say to yourself, "Here is room for mercy in me. If ever a soul wanted healing, I do. Here is space for divine power to operate in me, for if ever a soul was weak and palsied, I am just that soul." Be cheered with the hope that God will make of your infirmity a platform upon which He will display His power.

The man had been paralyzed *eight years*. The length of its endurance is a terrible element in a disease. Perhaps yours is no eight years malady, but twenty-eight, or thirty-eight, or forty-eight, or seventy-eight, perhaps, eighty-eight years have you been in bondage under it. Well, blessed be God, the number of years in which we have lived in sin cannot prevent the mercy of God in Christ Jesus from making us whole. You have a very long bill to discharge, while another friend has but a short one, and owes comparatively little; but it is just as easy for the creditor to write Paid at the bottom of the large bill as the smaller one. And now that our Lord Jesus Christ has made full atonement it is as easy for God to pardon the iniquities of eighty years as the sins of the child of eight. Be not despairing, then. Jesus Christ can make such as you are whole, even though your heart and your understanding have been long paralyzed with sin.

The man's disease was one which was then reckoned to be, and probably is now, *entirely incurable*. Who can restore a palsied person? Aeneas could not restore himself, and no merely human physician had skill to do anything for him. Dear hearer, has the Spirit of God made you feel that your soul's wound is incurable? Is your heart sick? Is your understanding darkened? Do you feel your whole nature to have become paralyzed with sin, and is there no physician? Ah, I know there is none among men and women, for there is no balm in Gilead, there is no physician there; there never was, or else the daughter of my people would have been healed of her hurt long ago. There is no soul physician except at Calvary; no balm but in the Savior's wounds. If you feel that you are incurably soul-sick, and the case is desperate unless infinite mercy shall interpose, then I am glad that you are here tonight. I am glad that there is such a one as Aeneas present. Do you know that the most delightful task in the world is to preach to those who consciously need the Savior? Mr. Whitfield used to say that he could wish to preach all day and all night long to those who really knew that they wanted Christ. We are bound to preach to everybody, for our Master said, "preach the gospel to every creature" under heaven. But, oh, when we can get at a knot of hungry souls it is easy and pleasant work to feed them with the bread of heaven; and when hearts are thirsty it is sweet work to hand out the living water, for they are all eager to take it. You know, the great difficulty is that you can bring a horse to the water, but you cannot make him drink if he is not thirsty. So you may set Jesus Christ before men and women, but if they do not feel their need of Him they will not have Him. You may preach in tones of thunder, or plead with accents of intense affection, but you cannot stir them to desire the grace which is in Christ Jesus, unless they feel their need of it. Oh, I am happy tonight—thrice happy—if anywhere in this house there is an Aeneas who is sick, and knows that he is sick; who knows his disease to be incurable, laments that he is palsied and can do nothing, and longs to be healed by divine power. He is the one who will welcome the glad news of the Gospel of free grace. The man was really sick, and so are you, my hearer; your sins are great, your sinfulness of nature is grievous, and your case is beyond reach of human skill.

He Knew Something About Jesus

In the second place, this man, Aeneas, knew something about Jesus because, otherwise, when Peter said, "Jesus Christ maketh thee whole," Aeneas might have earnestly inquired what he meant, but could not intelligently have acted upon what he could not comprehend. He could not have believed what Peter said because he would not have understood his meaning. Mere words, unless they appeal to the understanding, cannot be useful; they must convey light as well as sound, or they cannot breed faith. When Peter said, "Aeneas, Jesus Christ maketh thee whole," I have no doubt that Aeneas remembered what he had aforetime heard about Jesus Christ, and His wondrous life and death. Now, lest there should be one in this congregation who does not know Jesus Christ, and does not understand how it is that He is able to heal sin-sick souls, let us briefly tell the old, old story over again.

Jesus Christ, translated into English, means a "Savior anointed." Who is He? He is the Son of the Highest, very God of very God. When we were lost in sin, He who is called the Son of God laid aside His most divine array, and came hither to be dressed like ourselves in this poor flesh and blood. In the manger He lay as an infant, and on a woman's breast He hung a feeble babe. The God who stretched forth the heavens like a tent to dwell in and dug the deep foundations of the earth, came down to earth to take upon Himself our nature and to be born of a woman. Oh, matchless stoop of unbounded condescension that the Infinite should be an infant, and the Eternal God should conceal Himself within the form of a babe. This marvel was performed that we might be saved. Being here, the Lord of angels lived some thirty years or so among humanity. He spent the earliest part of His life as a carpenter's son obedient to His father, and He was throughout the whole of His earthly sojourn obedient to His Father, God. Inasmuch as we had no righteousness, for we had broken the law, He was here to make a righteousness for us, and He did so. But there was also wanted an atonement, for we had sinned, and God's judgment demanded that there should be punishment for sin. Jesus stepped in as the Surety and the Substitute for the guilty sons of men. He bared His book to the lash of justice, and opened His breast to her lance, and died that sinners might live. The just for the unjust, He died that He might bring us to God—

> He bore, that we might never bear,
> His Father's righteous ire.

Now, when He had thus lived and died, they placed His body in the tomb; but He rose again on the third day, and He is yet alive. By this man Christ Jesus, who is risen from the dead, is preached to the nations the remission of sins. For after forty days this same Jesus, who had been dead and buried, rose into the heavens in the presence of His disciples, ascending until a cloud concealed Him from their sight. He now sits at the right hand of God, even the Father, pleading there the merit of His blood, making intercession for sinners that they may be reconciled to God. Now, brothers and sisters, this is the story that we have to tell you, with the addition that this same Jesus is coming again to judge the living and the dead, for He is Lord of all. He is at this hour the Mediator appointed by the infinitely glorious Jehovah, having power over all flesh that He may give eternal life to as many as Jehovah has given Him. This we beseech you to consider, lest when He comes as a judge you should be condemned at His bar. Aeneas had heard more or less of these great facts. The story of the incarnate God had come to his ears by some means or other, and Aeneas understood that though Jesus Christ was not in the room, and there was only Peter and a few friends there, and though Jesus Christ was not on earth, but was gone to heaven, yet His power on earth was the same as ever it was. He knew that Jesus could work miracles from heaven as well as when He was here below. He understood that He who healed the palsy when He was here, could heal the palsy now that He has risen to His throne; so Aeneas believed in Jesus Christ from what he had heard, simply trusting in Him for healing. By means of that faith Aeneas was made whole.

I will very earnestly dwell on that point for a second or two. I am persuaded that in this congregation all of you know the story of Jesus Christ crucified. You have heard it on the Sabbath from the pulpit. Your children sing it when they come home from the Sunday school. You have a Bible in every house, and you read the "old, old story" in the plain but sublime language of our own noble version. But, oh, if you have heard it and know it, how is it that you have not drawn from it the same inference that this poor paralyzed man did? How is it that you have no faith? Jesus lives, He sits on Zion's hill, He receives poor sinners still. Jesus lives "exalted on high to be a Prince and a Savior, to give repentance unto Israel and remission of sins." He can heal you now, and save you now as well as if you met Him in the street or saw Him standing at your door knocking for admittance. I would to God that this inference were drawn by you all.

He Believed on the Lord Jesus

We have got so far: the man was sick, and the man knew something about Christ. And now came the most important point of all: the man believed on the Lord Jesus.

Peter said to him, "Aeneas, Jesus Christ maketh thee whole." The man did not believe in Peter as the healer, for you notice Peter does not say anything about himself. Peter does not say, "As the head of the church, I, by power delegated to me, make you whole." There is no allusion to any such claim, Peter preached too clear a Gospel for that. That is the purest Gospel which has the least of man in it, and the most of Christ. I charge you, men and women, do not listen to that teaching which sets the priest in front of the Savior, or even by the side of the Savior, for it is false and ruinous. Your forefathers, Englishmen, your forefathers bled and died that they might never submit to that vile superstition which is being now propagated by a considerable party in the Established Church of this once Protestant land! No one beneath the sky has any more power to save your soul than you have yourself; if any presumptuous priestling tells you that he has, do not believe him, but despise his claims. An old woman asks me to cross her hand with a sixpence, and says that she will tell my fortune. I am not such a fool. And if another person dressed in habiliments, which are not quite so becoming to him as a red cloak is to an old woman, tells me that he can regenerate my child, or forgive my sins, I treat him with the same contempt and pity as that with which I treat the wicked hag. I believe in neither the one impostor nor the other. If ever you are saved you must be saved by Jesus Christ alone through your own personal belief in Him. Certainly not by the intervention of any person, or set of persons, hail they from whatever church they will. God send that the pope and the priesthood and all their detestable deceits may go down in this land and that Christ may be exalted.

As this man had no faith in any supposed power coming from Peter, much less had he any faith in himself, neither did he look within himself for hope. He did not say to Peter, "But I do not feel strength enough to get well." Neither did he say, "I think I do feel power enough to shake off this palsy." He said neither the one nor the other. Peter's message took him off from himself. It was, "Aeneas, *Jesus Christ* makes you whole. It is not that you have stamina in your constitution and rallying points about your bodily system. No, Aeneas, you are paralyzed; you can do nothing. But Jesus Christ makes you whole." That was what the man had to believe, and it is very much what you also, my dear hearer, must believe.

With his faith Aeneas had the desires which showed that it was not mere speculation, but solid practical believing. He anxiously wished to be made whole. Oh, that sinners anxiously wished to be saved! Oh, that yonder angry man wished to be cured of his bad temper! Oh, that yonder covetous woman wished to be cured of her avarice! Oh, that yonder lustful man wished to be cured of his uncleanness! Oh, that yon drunkard wished to be cured of his excess! Oh, that people really wanted to get rid of their sins! But no. I never heard of anyone reckoning a cancer to be a jewel, but there are many who look upon their sins as if they were gems, which they keep as hid treasure, so that they will sooner lose heaven than part with their lustful pleasures. Aeneas wanted to be made whole and was ready to believe when Peter spoke to him about Jesus Christ.

And what did Aeneas believe? He believed—and may you believe the same—first, that Jesus could heal *him*, could heal *him*, *Aeneas*. John Brown, do you believe that Jesus Christ can cure you? I do not care, John, what your faith is about your wife's case; it is about yourself that you want faith. Jesus Christ is able to save you—you, Aeneas; you, John Brown; you, Thomas; you, Sarah; you, Mary. He is able to save you. Can you grip that, and reply, "Yes, He is able to save *me*"?

And Aeneas believed that Jesus Christ was able to save him *there and then*, just as he was. He had not taken a course of physic; he had not been in physical training to strengthen his nerves and sinews and prepare him to be cured, but he believed that Jesus Christ could save him without any preparation, just as he was, then, immediately, with a present salvation. When you think what Christ is, and what He has done, it ought not to be difficult to believe this. But truly God's power must be revealed before your soul will believe this to salvation. Yet is it true that Jesus Christ can heal, and can heal at once. Whatever the sin is, He can cure it. I mentioned a whole set of sins just now. The scarlet fever of pride, the loathsome leprosy of lust, the shivering ague of unbelief, the paralysis of avarice—He can heal all, and with a word, instantaneously, forever, completely, just now. Yes, sinner, He can heal *you now*. Aeneas believed that. He believed, and, as he believed, Jesus did make him whole. Oh, I wish I could tonight so preach the Gospel that my Lord and Master would lead many unbelievers to believe in Him. O Holy Spirit, work with the Word! Sinner, do you want forgiveness? Christ has wrought it out. Every sin that you have done shall be forgiven you for His name's sake if you trust Jesus to do it. Do you see your sins like a great army pursuing you? Do you think they will swallow you up quick? Jesus Christ, if you believe in Him, will make an end of them all. You have read in Exodus how Pharaoh and his hosts pursued the tribes of Israel and the people were terribly alarmed; but early in the morning they were no more afraid, for Miriam took her timbrel, and the daughters of Israel went forth with her in the dance; and they sang, "Sing unto the Lord, for he hath triumphed gloriously. The horse and his rider hath he thrown into the sea." One of the most magnificent notes in that marvelous song was this, "The depths have covered them: there is not one of them left." The damsels took up the refrain, and sang, "Not one, not one, not one! The depths have covered them: there is not one of them left." Now, if you believe in Jesus, the whole army of your sins shall sink beneath the sea of His blood, and your soul shall sing, "The depths have covered them: there is not one of them left." Such shall be your song tonight, if you are enabled to believe in Jesus Christ, God's crucified Son.

But do not think that we preach about the pardon of past sin only, because if a someone could get his past sins pardoned and go on as he did before, it would be so much the worse for him. Pardon of sin, without deliverance from its power, would be rather a curse than a blessing; but wherever sin is pardoned, God breaks the neck of its power in the soul. Mind, we do not tell you that Jesus Christ will forgive the past and then leave you to live the same life as before. But we tell you this: whatever the sin is that is now a disease to you, Jesus Christ can heal you of it. He can save you from the habit and power of evil doing and thinking. I will not attempt to go into details. There are odd people coming into the Tabernacle on ordinary occasions, and so I dare say there may be tonight. How often has there come in a man to whom I might say, "Put out your tongue, sir. Ah, I see red spots and black spots for you are a liar and a swearer." Can my Master heal such a diseased tongue as that? Yes, trust Him tonight, and He will make you truthful, and purge you from your profanity. But here is another—I dare not describe him. Look at him! He has lived an unchaste life and strong are his passions; and he says, "Can I ever be recovered from my vile desires?" Oh, sir, my Lord can lay His hand on that hot heart of yours, and cool it down to a sweet sobriety of chastity. And you, fallen woman, do not think that you are beyond His powers; He shows Himself mighty to save such as "the woman that was a sinner." Ah, if you are a slave to vile sins, Jesus can give perfect freedom from vicious habits. You young man there, you know that you have fallen into many sins which you dare not mention, which coil about your heart and poison your life like serpents writhing within your conscience. My Lord can take them all out of the soul and deliver you from the results of their fiery venom. Yes, He can make you into a new creature and cause you to be born again. He can make you love the things that you once hated, and hate the things that you aforetime loved, and turn the current of your thoughts in quite another way. You see Niagara leaping down its awful height, and you say, "Who can stop this?" Ay, indeed, who can stop it? But my Master can, and if He speaks to the Niagara of your lust, and says, "Cease your raging!" it will pause at once. Yes, if He bids the waters of desire leap up instead of down, you shall be as full of love to Christ as once you were full of love to sin. He made the sun to stand still, and caused the moon to pause upon the hill of Gibeah; and He can do all things. Spoke He not the world out of nothing? And can He not create new hearts and right spirits in the souls of men and women who have been far off from Him by wicked works? He can do so, and blessed be His name He will. The world of mind is as much beneath His control as that of matter. If you believe, O sinner, to you I may say as Peter did to Aeneas, "Jesus Christ maketh thee whole."

He Was Healed

Well, now, let us pass on to notice, next, that the man was made whole. There was no imposture about it; he was made whole, and made whole there and then. Just fancy, for a minute, what would have been the result if he had not been made whole. What dishonor it would have been to Peter! Peter said, "Aeneas, Jesus Christ maketh thee whole": but there lies Aeneas as palsied as before. Everybody would say, "Peter is a false witness." Well now, I will not say that the preacher of the Gospel must see souls saved or else he is a false witness. I will not say that, but I will say that if ever my ministry, under God, does not save souls I will give it up. For it seems to me that if we do not bring souls to Christ we preachers are just good for nothing. What are we if we do not turn many to righteousness? Reapers who never reap, soldiers who never win a battle, fishermen who take no fish, and lights which enlighten no one. These are sad but true comparisons. Do I address any unsuccessful minister? I would not speak harshly to him, but I would speak very severely to myself if I were in his case. I remember the dream of a minister. He thought that he was in hell, and being there, he was dreadfully distressed, and cried out, "Is this the place where I am to be forever? I am a minister." A grim voice replied, "No, it is lower down for unfaithful ministers, much lower down than this." And then he awoke. Ah, and if we do not agonize until souls are brought to Christ, we shall have to agonize to all eternity. I am persuaded of it: we must have people saved, or else we shall be like Peter would have been if he had said, "Jesus Christ makes thee whole," and the man had not been made whole—we shall be dishonored witnesses.

What dishonor would have been brought upon the name of Jesus if the man had not been made whole. Suppose, my dear fellow sinner, you were to believe in Jesus Christ and yet were not saved; what then? Oh, I do not like to suppose so, for it is almost a blasphemy to imagine it, but yet consider it for a moment. Believe in Jesus and not be saved! Then He has broken His word, or lost His power to save, either of which we are unwilling to tolerate for a minute. If you believe in Jesus Christ, as surely as you live Jesus Christ has saved you. I will tell you one thing—if you believe in Jesus Christ and you are damned, I will be damned with you. Come! I will risk my soul on that bottom as surely as you will risk yours, for if the Lord Jesus Christ does ever lose a soul that trusts Him, He will lose mine. But He never will, He never can—

> His honor is engaged to save
> The meanest of his sheep:
> All that his heavenly Father gave,
> His hands securely keep.

Rest in Him and you shall be saved, else were His name dishonored.

And suppose that, like Aeneas, you trusted Christ—if you were not saved, what then? Why, then the Gospel would not be true. Shut up those churches, close those chapels, banish those ministers, burn those Bibles; there is no truth in any of them if a soul can believe in Jesus and yet not be saved. The Gospel is a lie, and an imposture, if it be true that any poor sinner can put his trust in Jesus and not be healed of his sins; for thus says the Lord of old, "Him that cometh to me I will in no wise cast out." This is His last word to His church, "Go ye into all the world and preach the gospel to every creature: he that believeth and is baptized shall be saved; he that believeth not shall be damned." If people believing are not saved from the power of sin, then the Gospel is not true, and we are sent on a fool's errand. But they *are* saved, blessed be the name of God, and the Gospel is truth itself.

Oh, my dear hearer, fain would I urge you to put your trust in Jesus Christ tonight, by the experience which I and other believers have enjoyed; for some of us have relied on the name of the Redeemer, and He has saved us. We shall never forget the day, some of us, when we left off self-righteousness and believed in Christ to the salvation of our souls. The marvel was done in a minute, but the change was so great that we can never explain it or cease to bless the Lord for it.

> Happy day! Happy day!
> When Jesus washed my sins away.

I recollect the morning when salvation came to me as I sat in a little Primitive Methodist chapel under the gallery, and the preacher said, "That young man looks unhappy"; and added, "Young man, you will never find peace except you look to Christ." He called out to me, "Look!" With a voice of thunder he shouted, "Young man, look! Look now!" I did look, I turned the eye of faith to Jesus at once. My burden disappeared, and my soul was merry as a bird let loose from her cage, even as it is now as often as I remember the blessed salvation of Jesus Christ. We speak what we do know; ours is no hearsay or second-hand testimony. We speak what we have felt and tasted and handled, and our anxiety is that you may know and feel the same. Remember, my dear hearer, that the way to use the Gospel is to put it to yourselves like this. What is your name? I said, "John Brown," just now, did I not? Suppose it is John Brown, then. Well, the Gospel says, "He that believeth on the Lord Jesus Christ hath everlasting life." Then it means, "If John Brown believes on Jesus he has everlasting life." "He that believeth and is baptized shall be saved"—"Then I, John Brown, believing and being baptized, shall be saved." Lay hold of it in that way.

Perhaps you say, "But may I put my name to a promise, and appropriate it in that fashion?" Yes, you may, because there is nothing in the Bible to say that your name was left out from the list of those to whom the promise is made. If I were a beggar in the streets and were very hungry, and I heard that there was a gentleman who was giving a good meal away, and that he had advertised that any beggar might come, I do not think I would say, "Well, my name is not down in his list." I would step away when I found that he inserted an excluding clause, "Charles Spurgeon shall not have any of the food I distribute," but not until then. Until I read in black and white that he excluded me I would run the risk and get in with the other hungry folk. Until he shut me out I would go. It should be his deed and not mine that kept me from the feast.

Sometimes you say, "But I am not fit to go to Christ." The fittest way to go to Christ is to go just as you are. What is the best livery to wear when you go begging? I recollect some long time ago when I lived not far from here, in the extremeness of my greenness, I gave a man who begged at the door a pair of patent leather boots. He put them on, and expressed great gratitude; but I met him afterward, and I was not at all surprised to find that he had pulled them off. They were not at all the style of things to go about begging in. People would look at him and say, "What! you needing coppers while wearing those handsome boots? Your tale won't do." A beggar succeeds a deal better barefoot than in fine shoes. Rags are the livery of mendicants. When you go and beg for mercy at the hand of God, do not put on those pretty righteousnesses of yours, but go with all your sin and misery, and emptiness, and wretchedness, and say, "Lord, here am I. You have said that Christ is able to save to the uttermost them that come to God by Him. I am a soul that wants saving to the uttermost, and here I am. I have come. Lord, save me."

Now, summing all up: this is what you have to do, sinner, in order to be saved tonight—simply believe in Jesus Christ. I saw a young woman from America in the vestry some little time ago who came in great concern of soul to know the way of salvation, and I said to her, "Do you not see it? If you trust Christ, you are saved." I quoted the Scriptures which teach this great truth and made them plain to her until the Holy Spirit opened her eyes; light came on her face in a moment, and she said, "I do see it. I trust Christ with all my heart; and I am to believe that I am saved because I trust Jesus, and He has promised to save believers?" "Yes," I replied, "you are getting on the rock now." "I feel," she said, "a deep peace beginning in my soul, but I cannot understand how it can be, for my grandfather belonged to the old school Presbyterians. He told me he was six years before he could get peace, and had to be put into a lunatic asylum, for he was so miserable." Ah, yes, I have no doubt such cases have happened. Some will go seventeen thousand miles round about merely to go across a street, but there is no need for it. There it is—"The word is upon you, on your lips and in your heart. If with your heart you will believe in the Lord Jesus Christ, and with your mouth make confession of Him, you shall be saved." There is nothing to be done; there is nothing to be felt; there is nothing to be brought. No preparation is wanted. Come just as you are and trust Christ to save you out and out this night, and you shall be saved. God's honor and Christ's word are pledged to it.

He Proved He Was Healed

This is the last thing. When Aeneas was healed he acted in conformity therewith. "Peter said unto him, Aeneas, Jesus Christ maketh thee whole: arise, and make thy bed." He did so. He rose directly and made his bed.

Now, if any of you say tonight, "I have believed in Jesus," remember you are bound to prove it. How prove it? Why, if you have believed in Jesus, you are made whole, and you are to go home and show people how whole you are. This man was palsied, and had been lying there prostrate eight years, and could never make his bed, but he proved he was healed by making his bed for himself. Perhaps here is a man who when he has entered his house has generally opened the door with an oath. If there is such a person here and Christ saves you He will wash your mouth out for you. You will have done with profane language forever. Your wife will be surprised, when you go home, to hear how differently you talk. Perhaps you have been used to mix with rough companions in your work, and you have talked as they have done. If Jesus Christ has made you whole, there is an end to all filthy speaking. Now you will talk graciously, sweetly, cleanly, profitably. In years gone by you were angry and passionate; if Jesus Christ has made you whole, you will be as tender as a lamb. You will find the old lion lifting his head and giving an occasional roar and a shake of his mane, but then he will be chained by the restraints of grace, while the meek and gentle lamb of the new nature will feed in pastures wide and green. Ah, if the Lord has saved you, the drunkard's bar stool will have no more of you, for you will want better company than the seats of scoffers can afford you. If the Lord saves you, you will want to do something for Him, to show your grateful love. I know this very night you will long to tell your children and tell your friends that Jesus Christ has made you whole. John Bunyan says that when he was made whole he wanted to tell the crows on the plowed land about it. I do not wonder that he did. Tell anything, tell everybody, "Jesus Christ has saved me." It is a sensation the like of which no one can imagine if he has not felt it, to be made a new creature right away, in a moment. That surprises all who see it, and as people like to tell news—strange news—so does a newborn person long to go and tell others, "I have been born again: I have found the Savior."

Now, mark, you will have to prove that this is so by an honest, upright, consistent, holy life—not, however, by being merely sternly honest. If Christ has saved you, He will save you from being selfish. You will love other people; you will desire to do them good. You will endeavor to help the poor; you will try to instruct the ignorant. He or she who truly becomes a Christian becomes in that very same day a practical philanthropist. No one is a true Christian who is un-Christlike—who can live for himself alone, to hoard money or to make himself great. The true Christian lives for others. In a word, he lives for Christ. If Christ has healed you, gentle compassion will saturate your soul from this time forth and forever. O Master, You who did heal people's bodies in the days of Your flesh, heal people's hearts tonight, we pray You.

Still this word more. Somebody says, "Oh, I wish I had Christ!" Soul, why not have Him at once? "Oh, but I am not fit." You never will be fit; you cannot be fit, except in the sense in which you are fit even now. What is fitness for washing? Why, being dirty. What is fitness for charity? Why, being in distress. What is fitness for a doctor? Why, being ill. This is all the fitness that anyone wants for trusting in Christ to save him. Christ's mercy is to be had for nothing, bribe or purchase is out of the question. I have heard of a woman whose child was in a fever and needed grapes, and there was a prince who lived near in whose hothouse there were some of the rarest grapes that had ever been grown. She scraped together the little money she could earn, and went to the gardener and offered to buy a bunch of the royal fruit. Of course he repulsed her, and said they were not to be sold. Did she imagine that the prince grew grapes to sell like a market gardener? And he sent her on her way much grieved. She came again; she came several times, for a mother's importunity is great. But no offer of hers would be accepted. At last the princess heard of it and wished to see the woman. When she came the princess said, "The prince does not sell the fruit of his garden." But, snipping off a bunch of grapes and dropping them into a little bag, she said, "He is always ready to give it away to the poor." Now, here is the rich cluster of Gospel salvation from the true vine. My Lord will not sell it, but He is always ready to give it away to all who humbly ask for it. If you want it, come and take it, and take it now by believing in Jesus.

    The Lord bless you for Christ's sake. Amen.

3

Nothing but Leaves

He found nothing but leaves (Mark 11:13).

Most of the miracles of Moses were grand displays of divine justice. What were the first ten wonders but ten plagues? The same may be said of the prophets, especially of Elijah and Elisha. Was it not significant both of the character and mission of Elias when he called fire from heaven upon the captains of fifties; nor was he upon whom his mantle descended less terrible when the she-bears avenged him upon the mockers. It remained for our incarnate Lord to reveal the heart of God. The Only Begotten was full of grace and truth, and in His miracles preeminently God is set forth to us as LOVE. With the exception of the miracle before us, and perhaps, a part of another, all the miracles of Jesus were entirely benevolent in their character; indeed this one is no exception in reality, but only in appearance. The raising of the dead, the feeding of the multitude, the stilling of the tempest, the healing of diseases—what were all these but displays of the lovingkindness of God? What was this to teach us but that Jesus Christ came forth from His Father on an errand of pure grace?

> Thine hands, dear Jesus, were not arm'd
>   With an avenging rod,
> No hard commission to perform
>   The vengeance of a God.
>
> But all was mercy, all was mild,
>   And wrath forsook the throne,
> When Christ on his kind errand came
>   And brought salvation down.

This sermon was taken from *The Metropolitan Tabernacle Pulpit* and was preached on Sunday morning, February 21, 1864.

Nothing but Leaves

Let us rejoice that God commends His love toward us, because in "due time Christ died for the ungodly."

Yet, as if to show that Jesus the Savior is also Jesus the Judge, one gleam of justice must dart forth. Where shall mercy direct its fall? See, my friends, it glances not upon a person, but lights upon an unconscious, unsuffering thing—a tree. The curse, if we may call it a curse at all, did not fall on human or beast, or even the smallest insect; its bolt falls harmlessly upon a fig tree by the wayside. It bore upon itself the signs of barrenness, and perhaps was no one's property; little, therefore, was the loss which anyone sustained by the withering of that verdant mockery, while instruction more precious than a thousand acres of fig trees has been left for the benefit of all ages. The only other instance at which I hinted just now was the permission given to the devils to enter into the swine, and the whole herd ran violently down a steep place into the sea, and perished in the waters. In that case, again, what a mercy it was that the Savior did not permit a band of people to become the victims of the Evil One. It was infinitely better that the whole herd of swine should perish than that one poor man should be rendered a maniac through their influence. The creatures choked in the abyss were nothing but swine—swine which their Jewish owners had no right to keep; and even then they did not perish through Jesus Christ's agency, but through the malice of the devils, for even swine must run when the Devil drives.

Observe, then, with attention, this solitary instance of stern judgment wrought by the Savior's hand. Consider seriously that if only once in His whole life Christ works a miracle of pure judgment, the lesson so unique must be very full of meaning. If there be but one curse, where does it fall? What is its symbolic teaching? I do not know that I ever felt more solemnly the need of true fruitfulness before God than when I was looking over this miracle-parable—for such it may justly be called. The curse, you at once perceive, falls in its metaphorical and spiritual meaning upon those high professors who are destitute of true holiness; upon those who manifest great show of leaves, but who bring forth no fruit to God. Only one thunderbolt, and that for boasting pretenders; only one curse, and that for hypocrites. O blessed Spirit, write this heart-searching truth upon our hearts!

Other Trees Had Only Leaves

It is the nature of many trees to yield to man nothing but their shade. The hungering Savior did not resort to the oak or to the elm to look for food; neither could the fir tree, nor the pine, nor the box offer Him any hope of refreshment; nor did He breathe one hard word concerning them, for He knew what was in them and that they neither were, nor pretended to be, fruit-bearing trees. So, dear friends, there are many people whose lives bear leaves, but no fruit—and yet, thanks be to God, almighty patience bears with them. They are allowed to live out their time, and then it is true they are cut down and cast into the fire; but while they are permitted to stand, no curse withers them. The longsuffering of God waits to be gracious to them. Here are some of the characters who have leaves but no fruit.

There are thousands who ignorantly follow *the sign and know nothing of the substance*. In England, we think ourselves far in advance of popish countries; but how much of the essence of popery peeps out in the worship of very many! They go to church or chapel, and they think that the mere going into the place and sitting a certain time and coming out again is an acceptable act to God—mere formality, you see, is mistaken for spiritual worship! They are careful to have their infants sprinkled, but what the ceremony means they know not; and without looking into the Bible to see whether the Lord commands any such an ordinance, they offer Him their ignorant will-worship either in obedience to custom, or in the superstition of ignorance. What the thing is, or why it is, they do not inquire, but go through a performance as certain parrots say their prayers. They know nothing about the inward and spiritual grace which the Catechism talks about, if indeed, inward spiritual grace could ever be connected with an unscriptural outward and visible sign. When these poor souls come to the Lord's Supper, their thoughts go no farther than the bread and wine, or the hands which break the one and pour out the other. They know nothing whatever of communion with Jesus, of eating His flesh and drinking His blood. Their souls have proceeded as far as the shell, but they have never broken into the kernel to taste the sweetness thereof. They have a name to live and are dead. Their religion is a mere show; a signboard without an inn; a well-set table without meat; a pretty pageant where nothing is gold, but everything gilt; nothing real, but all pasteboard, paint, plaster, and pretense. Nonconformists, your chapels swarm with such, and the houses of the Establishment are full of the same! Multitudes live and die satisfied with the outward trappings of religion and are utter strangers to internal vital godliness. Yet such persons are not cursed in this life! No, they are to be pitied, to be prayed for, be sought after with words of love and honest truth; they are to be hoped for yet, for who knows but that God may call them to repent and they may yet receive the life of God into their souls?

Another very numerous class have *opinion but not faith*, creed but not credence. We meet them everywhere. How zealous they are for Protestantism! They would not only die for orthodoxy, but kill others as well. Perhaps it is the Calvinistic doctrine which they have received, and then the five points are as dear to them as their five senses. These people will contend, not to say earnestly, but savagely for the faith. They very vehemently denounce all those who differ from them in the smallest degree. They deal damnation around the land with amazing liberality to all who are not full weight according to the balance of their little Zoar, Rehoboth, or Jireh. While all the while the spirit of Christ, the love of the Spirit, hearts of compassion, and holiness of character are no more to be expected from them than grapes from thorns, or figs from thistles. Doctrine, my brethren, is to be prized above all price! Woe to the church of God when error shall be thought a trifle, for truth will be lightly esteemed; and when truth is gone, what is left? But, at the same time, we grossly mistake if we think that orthodoxy of creed will save us. I am sick of those cries of "the truth," "the truth," "the truth," from those of rotten lives and unholy tempers. There is an orthodox as well as a heterodox road to hell, and the Devil knows how to handle Calvinists quite as well as Arminians. No precinct of any church can insure salvation, no form of doctrine can guarantee to us eternal life. "Ye must be born again." You must bring forth fruits meet for repentance "Every tree which bringeth not forth fruit is hewn down, and cast into the fire." Stopping short of vital union to the Lord Jesus by real faith, we miss the great qualification for entering heaven. Yet the time is not come when these mere head-knowers are cursed. These trees have leaves only, but no fatal curse has withered them hopelessly. No; they are to be sought after. They may yet know the Lord in their hearts, and the Holy Spirit may yet make them humble followers of the Lamb. O that it may be so!

A third class have *talk without feeling*. Mr. Talkative, in *Pilgrim's Progress*, is the representative of a very numerous host. They speak very glibly concerning divine things. Whether the topic be doctrinal, experimental, or practical, they talk fluently upon everything. But evidently, the whole thing comes from the throat and the lips; there is no welling up from the heart. If the thing came from the heart it would be boiling, but now it hangs like an icicle from their lips. You know them—you may learn something from them, but all the while you are yourself aware that if they bless others by their words, they themselves remain unblessed. Ah! let us be very anxious lest this should be our own case. Let the preacher feel the anxiety of the apostle Paul, lest, after having preached to others, he himself should be a castaway. Let my hearers feel the same concern, lest, after talking about the things of God, they should prove to be mere lip-servers, and not accepted children of the Most High.

Another tribe springs up just now before my eyes—those who have *regrets without repentance*. Many of you under a heart-searching sermon feel grieved on account of your sins, and yet never have the strength of mind to give them up. You say you are sorry, but yet go on in the same course. You do really feel, when death and judgment press upon you, a certain sort of regret that you could have been so foolish, but the next day the strength of temptation is such that you fall a prey to the very same infatuation. It is easy to bring a person to the river of regret, but you cannot make him drink the water of repentance. If Agag would be killed with words, no Amalekite would live. If people's transient sorrows for sin were real repentance on account of it, there is not anyone living who would not, sometime or other, have been a true penitent. Here, however, are leaves only, and no fruit.

We have yet again, another class of persons who have *resolves without action*. They *will*! Ah! that they *will*! But it is always in the future tense. They are hearers, and they are even feelers, but they are not doers of the Word. It never comes to that. They would be free, but they have no patience to file their fetters, nor grace to submit their manacles to the hammer. They see the right, but they permit the wrong to rule them. They are charmed with the beauties of holiness, and yet deluded with the wantonness of sin. They would run in the ways of God's commandments, but the road is too rough, and running is weary work. They would fight for God, but victory is hard to win, and so they turn back almost as soon as they have set out; they put their hand to the plow, and then prove utterly unworthy of the kingdom.

The great majority of persons who have any sort of religion at all bear leaves, but they produce no fruit. I know there are some such here, and I solemnly warn you, though no curse falls upon you, though we do not think that the miracle now under consideration has any relation to you whatever, yet remember, there is nothing to be done with trees which bring forth only leaves, but in due time to use the ax upon them and to cast them into the fire. *This must be your doom*. As sure as you live under the sound of the Gospel and yet are not converted by it, so surely will you be cast into outer darkness. As certainly as Jesus Christ invites you and you will not come, so certainly will He send His angels to gather the dead branches together, and you among them, to cast them into the fire. Beware! beware! you fruitless tree! you shall not stand forever! Mercy waters you with her tears now; God's loving-kindness digs about you still; still the husbandman comes, seeking fruit upon you year after year. Beware! the edge of the ax is sharp, and the arm which wields it is nothing less than almighty. Beware! lest you fall into the fire!

There Were Other Trees with Neither Leaves nor Fruit, and None of These Were Cursed

The time of figs was not yet come. Now, as the fig tree either brings forth the fig before the leaf or else produces figs and leaves at the same time, the major part of the trees, perhaps all of them, without exception of this one, were entirely without figs and without leaves, and yet Jesus did not curse any one of them, for the time of figs was not yet come. What multitudes are destitute of anything like religion? They make no profession of it. They not only have no fruits of godliness but they have no leaves even of outward respect to it. They do not frequent the court of the Lord's house. They use no form of prayer; they never attend upon ordinances. The great outlying mass of this huge city—how does religion affect it? It is a very sad thing to think that there are people living in total darkness next door to the light; that you may find in the very street where the Gospel is preached persons who have never heard a sermon. Are there not, throughout this city, tens and hundreds of thousands who know not their right hand from their left in matters of godliness? Their children go to Sabbath schools, but they themselves spend the whole Sabbath day in anything except the worship of God! In our country parishes, very often neither the religion of the Establishment nor of Dissent at all affects the population. Take, for instance, that village which will be disgracefully remembered as long as Essex endures, the village of Hedingham. There are in that place not only parish churches, but Dissenting meeting houses, and yet the persons who foully murdered the poor wretch supposed to be a wizard must have been as ignorant and indifferent to common sense, let alone religion, as even Hottentots or Kafirs, to whom the light of religion has never come. Why was this? Is it not because there is not enough of missionary spirit among Christian people to seek out those who are in the lowest strata of society, so that multitudes escape without ever coming into contact with godliness at all? In London, the City Missionaries will hear witness that while they can sometimes meet with the wives, yet there are thousands of husbands who are necessarily away at the time of the missionary's visit, who have not a word of rebuke, or exhortation, or invitation, or encouragement ever sounding in their ears at all, from the day of their birth to the day of their death. They might, for all practical purposes, as well have been born in the center of Africa as in the city of London, for they are without God, without hope, aliens from the commonwealth of Israel, far off, not by wicked works only, but by dense ignorance of God.

These persons we may divide into two classes, upon neither of whom does the withering curse fall in this life. The first we look upon with hope. Although we see neither leaves nor fruit, we know that "the time of figs is not yet." They are God's *elect*, but they are *not called*. Their names are in the Lamb's Book of Life and were there from before the foundations of the world. Though they be dead in trespasses, they are the objects of divine love, and *they must*, in due time, be called by irresistible grace and turned from darkness to light. "The Lord hath much people in this city," and this should be the encouragement of every one of you to try to do good, that God has among the vilest of the vile, the most reprobate, the most debauched and drunken, an elect people who *must* be saved. When you take the Word to them, you do so because God has ordained you to be the messenger of life to their souls, and they *must* receive it, for so the decree of predestination runs; they must be called in the fullness of time to be the brothers and sisters of Christ and children of the Most High. They are *redeemed*, beloved friends, but *not regenerated*—as much redeemed with precious blood as the saints before the eternal throne. They are Christ's property, and yet perhaps, they are waiting around the tavern at this very moment until the door shall open—bought with Jesus' precious blood, and yet spending their nights in a brothel, and their days in sin. But if Jesus Christ purchased them He will have them. If He counted down the precious drops, God is not unfaithful to forget the price which His Son has paid. He will not suffer His substitution to be in any case an ineffectual, dead thing. Tens of thousands of redeemed ones are not regenerated yet, but regenerated they must be; and this is your comfort and mine, when we go out with the quickening Word of God. No, more, these ungodly ones are prayed for by Christ before the throne. "Neither pray I for these alone," says the great Intercessor, "but for *them also which shall believe* on me through their word." They do not pray for themselves; poor, ignorant souls, they do not know anything about prayer; but Jesus prays for them. Their names are on His breast, and before long they must bow the stubborn knee, breathing the penitential sigh before the throne of grace. "The time of figs is not yet." The predestinated moment has not struck; but, when it comes, *they shall,* for God will have His own. *They must,* for the Spirit is not to be withstood when He comes forth with power—*they must* become the willing servants of the living God. "My people shall be willing in the day of my power." "He shall justify many." "He shall see of the travail of his soul." "He shall divide a portion with the great, and he shall divide the spoil with the strong."

No curse falls upon these; they deserve it, but eternal love prevents it. Their sins write it, but the finished sacrifice blots it out. They may well perish because they seek not mercy, but Christ intercedes for them, and live they shall.

Alas! however, among those who have neither leaves nor fruit, there is another class which *never* bring forth either the one or the other; they live in sin and die in ignorance, perishing without hope. As these leave the world, can they upbraid us for neglecting them? Are we clear of their blood? May not the blood of many of them cry from the ground against us? As they are condemned on account of sins, may they not accuse us because we did not take the Gospel to them, but left them where they were? Dread thought! but let it not be shaken off. There are tens of thousands every day who pass into the world of spirits unsaved, and inherit the righteous wrath of God. Yet in this life, you see, no special curse falls upon them, and this miracle has no special bearing upon them; it bears upon a totally different class of people, of whom we will now speak.

Fig Trees Bear Fruit Before Leaves

I have already said that in a fig tree the fruit takes the precedence of the leaves, or the leaves and the fruit come at the same time, so that it is laid down as a general rule that if there are leaves upon a fig tree, you may rightly expect to find fruit upon it.

To begin then with the explanation of this special case, *in a fig tree fruit comes before leaves*. So in a true Christian, fruit always takes the precedence of profession. Find a person anywhere who is a true servant of God, and before he united himself with the church, or attempted to engage in public prayer, or to identify himself with the people of God, he searched to see whether he had real repentance on account of sin. He desired to know whether he had a sincere and genuine faith in the Lord Jesus Christ, and he perhaps tarried some little time to try himself to see whether there were the fruits of holiness in his daily life. Indeed, I may say that there are some who wait too long. They are so afraid lest they should make a profession before they have grace in possession that they will wait year after year—too long—become unwise, and make what was a virtue become a vice. Still this is the rule with Christians: they first give themselves to the Lord and afterward to the Lord's people according to His will. You who are the servants of God—do you not scorn to vaunt yourselves beyond your reach? Would you not think it disgraceful on your part to profess anything which you have not felt? Do you not feel a holy jealousy when you are teaching others, lest you should teach more than God has taught you? and are you not afraid even in your prayers lest you should use expressions which are beyond your own depth of meaning? I am sure the true Christian is always afraid of anything like having the leaves before he or she has the fruit.

Another remark follows from this—*where we see the leaves we have a right to expect the fruit*. When I see a man a church member, when I hear him engage in prayer, I expect to see in him holiness, the character and the image of Christ. I have a right to expect it because the man has solemnly avowed that he is the partaker of divine grace. You cannot join a church without taking upon yourselves very solemn responsibilities. What do you declare when you come to see us and ask to be admitted into fellowship? You tell us that you have passed from death to life, that you have been born again, that there has been a change in you, the like of which you never knew before, one which only God could have wrought. You tell us you are in the habit of private prayer; that you have a desire for the conversion of others. If you did not so profess, we dare not receive you. Well now, having made these professions, it would be insincere on our part if we did not expect to see your characters holy, and your conversation correct. We have a right to expect it from your own professions. We have a right to expect it from the work of the Spirit which you claim to have received. Shall the Holy Spirit work in a person's heart to produce a trifle? Do you think that the Spirit of God would have written us this Book, and that Jesus Christ would have shed His precious blood to produce a hypocrite? Is an inconsistent Christian the highest work of God? I suppose God's plan of salvation to be that which has more exercised His thoughts and wisdom than the making of all worlds and the sustenance of all providence; and shall this best, this highest, this darling work of God, produce no more than that poor, mean, talking, unacting, fruitless deceiver? You have no love for souls, no care for the spread of the Redeemer's kingdom, and yet think that the Spirit has made you what you are! No zeal, no melting hearts of compassion, no cries of earnest entreaty, no wrestling with God, no holiness, no self-denial, and yet say that you are a vessel made by the Master and fitted for His use! How can this be? No; if you profess to be a Christian, from the necessity of the Spirit's work, we have a right to expect fruit from you. Besides, in genuine professors we do get the fruit, we see a faithful attachment to the Redeemer's cause, an endurance to the end, in poverty, in sickness, in shame, in persecution. We see other professors holding fast to the truth; they are not led aside by temptation, neither do they disgrace the cause they have espoused; if you profess to be one of the same order, we have a right to look for the same blessed fruits of the Spirit in you, and if we see them not you have belied us.

Observe further that *our Lord hungers for fruit*. A hungry person seeks for something which may satisfy him, for fruit, not leaves! Jesus hungers for your holiness. A strong expression, you will say, but I doubt not of its accuracy. For what were we elected? We were predestinated to be conformed to the image of God's Son. We were chosen to good works, "which God hath before ordained that we should walk in them." What is the end of our redemption? Why did Jesus Christ die? "He gave himself for us that he might redeem us from all iniquity, and purify unto himself a peculiar people, zealous of good works." Why have we been called but that we should be called to be saints? To what end are any of the great operations of the covenant of grace? Do they not all point at our holiness? If you will think of any privilege which the Lord confers upon His people through Christ, you will perceive that they all

Nothing but Leaves

aim at the sanctification of the chosen people—the making of them to bring forth fruit that God the Father may be glorified in them. O Christian, for this the tears of the Savior! for this the agony and bloody sweat! for this the five death wounds! for this the burial and the resurrection, that He make you holy, even perfectly holy like to Himself! And can it be, that when He hungers after fruit, you think nothing of bearing fruit? O professor, how base are you, to call yourself a blood-bought child of God, and yet to live to yourself! How dare you, O barren tree, professing to be watered by the bloody sweat, and dug by the griefs and woes of the wounded Savior—how dare you bring forth leaves and no fruit? Oh! sacrilegious mockery of a hungry Savior! oh! blasphemous tantalizing of a hungry Lord! that you should profess to have cost Him all this, and yet yield Him nothing! When I think that Jesus hungers after fruit in me, it stirs me up to do more for Him. Does it not have the same effect on you? He hungers for your good works; He hungers to see you useful. Jesus the King of Kings hungers after your prayers—hungers after your anxieties for the souls of others, and nothing ever will satisfy Him for the travail of His soul but seeing you wholly devoted to His cause.

This brings us into the very midst and meaning of the miracle. *There are some, then, who make unusual profession, and yet disappoint the Savior in His just expectations.* The Jews did this. When Jesus Christ came it was not the time of figs. The time for great holiness was after the coming of Christ and the pouring out of the Spirit. All the other nations were without leaves. Greece, Rome, all these showed no signs of progress; but there was the Jewish nation covered with leaves. They professed already to have obtained the blessings which He came to bring. There stood the Pharisee with his long prayers; there were the lawyers and the scribes with their deep knowledge of the things of the kingdom. They said they had the light. The time of figs was not come; but they had the leaves, though not a single fruit. You know what a curse fell on Israel; how in the day of Jerusalem's destruction the tree was withered altogether from its root because it had its leaves but had no fruit.

The same will be true of any *church*. There are times when all the churches seem sunken alike in lethargy—such a time we had, say ten years ago—but one church, perhaps, seems to be all alive. The congregations are large. Much, apparently, is proposed for the growth of the Savior's kingdom. A deal of noise is made about it. There is much talk, and the people are all expectation. If there be no fruit, no real consecration to Christ, if there be no genuine liberality, no earnest vital godliness, no hallowed consistency, other churches may live on; but such a church as this, making so high a profession and being so precocious in the produce of leaves, shall have a curse from God. No one shall eat fruit of it forever, and it shall wither away.

In the case of *individuals* the moral of our miracle runs thus. Some are looked upon as *young believers* who early join the church. "The time of figs is not yet"; it is not a very ordinary case to see children converted, but we do see some, and we are very grateful. We are jealous, however, lest we should see leaves but not fruit. These juveniles are extraordinary cases, and on that account we look for higher results. When we are disappointed what shall come upon such but a curse upon their precocity, which led them to the deception. Some of us were converted, or profess to have been, when young, and if we have lived hitherto, and all we have produced has been merely words, resolves, professions, but not fruit to God, we must expect the curse.

Again, *professors eminent in station*. There are necessarily but few ministers, but few church officers; but when people so distinguish themselves by zeal, or by louder professions than others, as to gain the ear of the Christian public and are placed in responsible positions—if they bring forth no fruit, they are the persons upon whom the curse will light. It may be with other Christians that "the time of figs is not yet." They have not made the advances which these profess to have made; but having been, upon their own profession, elected to an office which essentially requires fruit, since they yield it not, let them beware.

To those who make professions of much love to Christ, the same caution may be given. With the most of Christians, I am afraid, I must say that "the time of figs is not yet," for we are too much like the Laodicean church. But you meet with some people—how much they are in love with Christ. How sweetly they can talk about Him, but what do they do for Him? Nothing! nothing! Their love lies just in the wind which comes out of their own mouths, and that is all. Now when the Lord has a curse, He will deal it out on such. They went beyond all others in an untimely declaration of a very fervent love, and now they yield Him no fruit. "Yes," said one, "I love God so much that I do not reckon that anything I have is my own. It is all the Lord's—all the Lord's, and I am His steward." Well, this dear good man, of course, joined the church, and after a time, some mission work wanted a little help. What was his reply? "When I pay my seat rent, I have done all I intend to do." A man of wealth and means! After a little time, this same man found it inconvenient even to pay for his seat and goes now to a place not quite so full where he can get a seat and do nothing to support the ministry! If there is a special thunderbolt anywhere, it is these unctuous hypocrites who whine about love to Christ, and bow down at the shrine of mammon.

Or, take another case. You meet with others whose profession is not of so much love, but it is of *much experience*. Oh! what experience they have had! What deep experience! Ah! they know the humblings of heart and the plague of human nature! They know the depths of corruption, and the heights of divine fellowship, and so on. Yes, and if you go into the shop you find the corruption is carried on behind the counter, and the deceit in the daybook; if they do not know the plague of their own hearts, at least they are a plague to their own household. Such people are abhorrent to all, and much more to God.

Others you meet with *who have a censorious tongue*. What good people they must be; they can see the faults of other people so plainly! This church is not right, and the other is not right, and yonder preacher—well some people think him a very good man, but they do not. They can see the deficiencies in the various denominations, and they observe that very few really carry out Scripture as it should be carried out. They complain of want of love and are the very people who create that want. Now if you will watch these very censorious people, the very faults they indicate in others they are inducing in themselves; and while they are seeking to find out the mote in their brother's eye, they have a beam in their own. These are the people who are indicated by this fig tree; they ought, according to their own showing, taking them on their own ground, to be better than other people. If what they say is true, they are bright particular stars, and they ought to give special light to the world. They are such that even Jesus Christ Himself might expect to receive fruit from them, but they are nothing but deceivers with these high soarings and proud boastings; they are nothing after all but pretenders. Like Jezebel with her paint, which made her all the uglier, they would seem to be what they are not. As old Adam says, "They are candles with big wicks and no tallow, and when they go out they make a foul and nauseous smell." "They have summer sweating on their brow, and winter freezing in their hearts." You would think them the land of Goshen, but prove them the wilderness of sin. Let us search ourselves lest such be the case with us.

Such a Tree Might Well Be Withered

Deception is abhorred of God. There was the Jewish temple, there were the priests standing in solemn pomp, there were the abundant sacrifices of God's altar. But was God pleased with His temple? No, because in the temple you had all the leaves. You had all the externals of worship, but there was no true prayer. No belief in the great Lamb of God's Passover, no truth, no righteousness, no love of the people, no care for the glory of God. So the temple, which had been a house of prayer, had become a den of thieves. You do not marvel that the temple was destroyed. You and I may become just like that temple. We may go on with all the externals of religion nobody may miss us out of our seat at Tabernacle. No, we may never miss our Christian engagements; we may be in all external matters more precise than we used to be, and yet for all that, we may have become in our hearts a den of thieves; the heart may be given to the world while external ceremonies are still kept up and maintained. Let us beware of this, for such a place cannot be long without a curse. It is abhorrent to God.

Again, *it is deceptive to man*. Look at that temple! What do people go there for? To see holiness and virtue. Why tread they its hallowed courts? To get nearer to God. And what do they find there? Instead of holiness, covetousness; instead of getting nearer to God, they get into the midst of a mart where men are haggling about the price of doves and bickering with one another about the changing of shekels. So others may watch to hear some seasonable word from our lips, and instead of that, may get evil; and as that temple was cursed for deluding people, so may we be, because we deceive and disappoint the wants of humanity.

More than this, this barren fig tree *committed sacrilege upon Christ*, did it not? Might it not have exposed Him to ridicule? Some might have said, "How do You go to a tree, You prophet, whereon there is no fruit?" A false professor exposes Christ to ridicule. As the temple of old dishonored God, so does a Christian when his heart is not right; he does dishonor to God, and makes the holy cause to be trodden under foot of the adversary. Such indviduals indeed have reason to beware.

Once more, this tree might well be cursed because its bringing forth nothing but leaves was a plain evidence of its sterility. It had force and vitality, but it turned it to ill account, and would continue to do so. The curse of Christ was but a confirmation of what it already was. He did as good as say, "He that is unfruitful, let him be unfruitful still." And now, what if Christ should come into this Tabernacle this morning, and should look on you and on me, and see in any of us great profession and great pomp of leaves, and yet no fruit. What if He should pronounce the curse on us, what would be the effect? We would wither away as others have done. What mean we by this? Why, they have on a sudden turned to the world. We could not understand why such fair saints should, on a sudden, become such black devils; the fact was, Christ had pronounced the word, and they began to wither away. If He should pronounce the unmasking word on any mere professor here, and say, "Let no man eat fruit of thee forever," you will go into gross outward sin and wither to your shame. This will take place probably on a sudden; and taking place, your case will be irretrievable; you never afterward will be restored. The blast which shall fall upon you will be eternal; you will live as a lasting monument of the terrible justice of Christ as the great Head of the church. You will be spared to let it be seen that a person outside the church may escape with impunity in this

Nothing but Leaves

life, but a person inside the church shall have a present curse and be made to stand as a tree blasted by the lightning of God forever.

Now, this is a heart-searching matter. It went through me yesterday when I thought, "Well, here am I, I have professed to be called of God to the ministry. I have forced myself into a leading place in God's church. I have voluntarily put myself into a place where sevenfold damnation is my inevitable inheritance if I am not true and sincere." I could almost wish myself back out of the church, or at least in the obscurest place in her ranks, to escape the perils and responsibilities of my position. So may you, if you have not the witness of the Spirit in you that you are born of God—you may wish that you never thought of Christ, and never dreamed of taking His name upon you. If you have by diligence worked yourself into a high position among God's people; if you have mere leaves without the fruit, the more sure is the curse, because the greater the disappointment of the Savior. The more you profess, the more is expected of you; and if you do not yield it, the more just the condemnation when you shall be left to stand forever withered by the curse of Christ. O men and women, let us tremble before the heart-searching eye of God; but let us still remember that grace can make us fruitful yet. The way of mercy is open still. Let us apply to the wounds of Christ this morning. If we have never begun, let us begin now. Now let us throw our arms about the Savior, and take Him to be ours; and, having done this, let us seek divine grace, that for the rest of our lives we may work for God. Oh! I do hope to do more for God, and I hope you will. O Holy Spirit, work in us mightily, for in You is our fruit found! Amen.

4

The Waterpots at Cana

Jesus saith unto them, Fill the waterpots with water. And they filled them up to the brim (John 2:7).

You know the narrative. Jesus was at a wedding feast, and when the wine ran short, He provided for it right bountifully. I do not think that I would do any good if I were to enter upon the discussion as to what sort of wine our Lord Jesus made on this occasion. It was wine, and I am quite sure it was very good wine, for He would produce nothing but the best. Was it wine such as people understand by that word now? It was wine; but there are very few people in this country who ever see, much less drink, any of that beverage. That which goes under the name of wine is not true wine, but a fiery, brandied concoction of which I feel sure that Jesus would not have tasted a drop. The firewaters and blazing spirits of modern wine manufacturers are very different articles from the juice of the grape, mildly exhilarating, which was the usual wine of more sober centuries. As to the wine such as is commonly used in the East, a person must drink inordinately before he would become intoxicated with it. It would be possible, for there were cases in which people were intoxicated with wine; but, as a rule, intoxication was a rare vice in the Savior's times and in the preceding ages. Had our great Exemplar lived under our present circumstances, surrounded by a sea of deadly drink which is ruining tens of thousands, I know how He would have acted. I am sure He would not have contributed by word or deed to the rivers of poisonous beverages in which bodies and souls are now being destroyed wholesale. The kind of wine which He made was such that, if there had been no stronger drink in the world, nobody might have thought it necessary to enter any protest against drinking it. It would

---

This sermon was taken from *The Metropolitan Tabernacle Pulpit* and was preached at the Metropolitan Tabernacle, Newington, in 1880.

The Waterpots at Cana

have done nobody any hurt, be sure of that, or else Jesus our loving Savior would not have made it.

Some have raised a question about the great quantity of wine, for I suppose there must have been no less than one hundred and twenty gallons, and probably more. "They did not want all that," says one, "and even of the weakest kind of wine it would be a deal too much." But you are thinking of an ordinary wedding here, are you not, when there are ten or a dozen, or a score or two, met together in a parlor? An oriental wedding is quite another affair. Even if it be only a village, like Cana of Galilee, everybody comes to eat and drink, and the feast lasts on for a week or a fortnight. Hundreds of people must be fed for often open house is kept. Nobody is refused, and consequently a great quantity of provision is required. Besides, they may not have consumed all the wine at once. When the Lord multiplied loaves and fishes, they must eat the loaves and fishes directly, or else the bread would grow moldy and the fish would be putrid; but wine could be stored and used months afterward. I have no doubt that such wine as Jesus Christ made was as good for keeping as it was for using. And why not set the family up with a store in hand? They were not very rich people. They might sell it if they liked. At any rate that is not my subject, and I do not intend getting into hot water over the question of cold water. I abstain myself from alcoholic drink in every form, and I think others would be wise to do the same; but of this each one must be a guide to himself.

Jesus Christ commenced the Gospel dispensation not with a miracle of vengeance, like that of Moses, who turned water into blood, but with a miracle of liberality, turning water into wine. He does not only supply necessaries, but gives luxuries, and this is highly significant of the kingdom of His grace. Here He not only gives sinners enough to save them, but He gives abundantly, grace upon grace. The gifts of the covenant are not stinted or stunted, they are neither small in quantity nor in quality. He gives to people not only the water of life that they may drink and be refreshed, but "wines on the lees well refined" that they may rejoice exceedingly. And He gives like a king, who gives lavishly, without counting the cups and bottles. As to one hundred and twenty gallons, how little is that in comparison with the rivers of love and mercy which He is pleased to bestow freely out of His bountiful heart upon the most needy souls. You may forget all about the wine question, and all about wine, bad, good, or indifferent. The less we have to do with it the better, I am quite sure. And now let us think about our Lord's mercy, and let the wine stand as a type of His grace, and the abundance of it as the type of the abundance of His grace which He does so liberally bestow.

Now, concerning this miracle, it may well be remarked how simple and unostentatious it was. One might have expected that when the great Lord of all came here in human form He would commence His miraculous career by summoning the scribes and Pharisees at least, if not the kings and princes of the earth, to see the marks of His calling and the guarantees and warrants of His commission, gathering them all together to work some miracle before them, as Moses and Aaron did before Pharaoh, that they might be convinced of His Messiahship. He does nothing of the kind. He goes to a simple wedding among poor people, and there in the simplest and most natural way He displays His glory. When the water is to be turned into wine, when He selects that as the first miracle, He does not call for the master of the feast even, or for the bridegroom himself, or for any of the guests, and begin to say, "You clearly perceive that your wine is all gone. Now, I am about to show you a great marvel, to turn water into wine." No, He does it quietly with the servants. He tells them to fill the waterpots. He uses the baths. He does not ask for any new vessels, but uses what were there, making no fuss or parade. He uses water, too, of which they had abundance, and works the miracle, if I may so speak, in the most commonplace and natural style; and that is just the style of Jesus Christ. Now, if it had been a Catholic miracle it would have been done in a very mysterious, theatrical, sensational way, with no end of paraphernalia; but being a genuine miracle it is done just as nearly after the course of nature as the supernatural can go. Jesus does not have the waterpots emptied and then fill them with wine, but He goes as far with nature as nature will go, and uses water to make the wine from, therein following the processes of His providence which are at work every day. When the water drops from heaven and flows into the earth to the roots of the vine, and so swells out the clusters with ruddy juice, it is through water that wine is produced. There is only a difference as to time whether the wine is created in the cluster or in the waterpots. Our Lord does not call for any strangers to do it, but the ordinary servants shall bring ordinary water. While they are drawing out the water, or what appears to them to be water, the servants shall perceive that the water has been turned into wine.

Now, whenever you try to serve Jesus Christ do not make a fuss about it, because He never made any fuss in what He did, even when He was working amazing miracles. If you want to do a good thing, go and do it as naturally as ever you can. Be simple-hearted and humble-minded. Be yourself. Do not be affected in your piety, as if you were going to walk to heaven on stilts. Walk on your own feet, and bring religion to your own door and to your own fireside. If you have a grand work to do, do it with that genuine simplicity which is next akin to sublimity; for affectation, and everything that is gaudy and ostentatious, is,

The Waterpots at Cana

after all, mean and beggarly. Nothing but simple naturalness has about it a genuine beauty, and such a beauty there is about this miracle of the Savior.

Let all these remarks stand as a kind of preface, for now I want to draw out *the principles which are hidden in my text*; and then, secondly, when I have displayed those principles, I want to show *how they should be carried out.*

What Are the Principles Involved in Our Lord's Mode of Procedure?

First, that, as a rule, *when Christ is about to bestow a blessing He gives a command.* This is a fact which your memories will help you to establish in a moment. It is not always so; but, as a general rule, a word of command goes before a word of power, or else with it. He is about to give wine, and the process does not consist in saying, "Let wine be," but it begins by a command addressed to people—"Fill the waterpots with water." Here is a blind man: Christ is about to give him sight. He puts clay on his eyes, and then says, "Go to the pool of Siloam and wash." There is a man with his arm swinging at his side, useless to him: Christ is going to restore it, and He says, "Stretch forth thine hand." Ay, and the principle goes so far that it holds good in cases where it would seem to be quite inapplicable, for if it is a child that is dead He says, "Maid, arise"; or if it be Lazarus, who by this time stinks, being four days buried, yet He cries, "Lazarus, come forth." And thus He bestows a benefit by a command. Gospel benefits come with a Gospel precept.

Do you wonder that this principle which is seen in the miracles is seen in the wonders of His divine grace? Here is a sinner to be saved. What does Christ say to that sinner? "Believe in the Lord Jesus Christ, and thou shalt be saved." Can he believe of himself? Is he not dead in sin? Friends, raise no such questions, but learn that Jesus Christ has bidden people believe, and has commissioned His disciples to cry, "Repent ye, for the kingdom of heaven is at hand." "The times of this ignorance God winked at; but now commandeth all men everywhere to repent." And He bids us go and preach this word—"Believe in the Lord Jesus Christ, and thou shalt be saved." But why command them? It is His will to do so, and that should be enough for you who call yourself His disciple. It was so even in the olden times when the Lord set forth in vision His way of dealing with a dead nation. There lay the dry bones in the valley, exceeding many, and exceeding dry, and Ezekiel was sent to prophesy to them. What said the prophet? "O ye dry bones, hear the word of the Lord." Is that his way of making them alive? Yes, by a command to hear—a thing which dry bones cannot do. He issues his command to the dead, the dry, the helpless, and by its power life comes. I pray you, be not disobedient to the Gospel, for faith is a duty, or we would not read of "the obedience of faith." Jesus Christ, when He is about to bless, challenges people's obedience by issuing His royal orders.

The same thing is true when we come away from the unconverted to believers. When God means to bless His people and make them blessings, it is by issuing a command to them. We have been praying to the Lord that He would arise and make bare His arm. His answer is, "Awake, awake, O Zion." We ask that the world may be brought to His feet, and His reply is, "All power is given unto me in heaven and in earth. Go ye therefore, and teach all nations, baptizing them." The command is to us the vehicle of the blessing. If we are to have the blessing of converts multiplied and churches built up, Christ must give us the boon. It is altogether His gift, as much as it was His to turn the water into wine; yet first of all He says to us, "Go ye and proclaim My salvation unto the ends of the earth," for thus are we to fill the waterpots with water. If we are obedient to His command we shall see how He will work—how mightily He will be with us, and how our prayers shall be heard.

That is the first principle that I see here: Christ issues commands to those whom He will bless.

Secondly, *Christ's commands are not to be questioned, but to be obeyed*. The people want wine, and Christ says, "Fill the waterpots with *water*." Well, now, if these servants had been of the mind of the captious critics of modern times, they would have looked at our Lord a long while and objected boldly: "We do not want any water. It is not the feast of purifications; it is a wedding feast. We do not require water at a wedding. We shall want water when we are going up to the synagogue or to the temple that we may purify our hands according to our custom. But we do not want water just now; the hour, the occasion, and the fitness of things call for *wine*." But Mary's advice to them was sound— "Whatsoever he saith to you, do it." Thus, too, let us neither question nor cavil, but do His bidding straightaway.

It may sometimes seem that Christ's command is not pertinent to the point in hand. The sinner, for instance, says, "Lord, save me; conquer in me my sin." Our Lord cries, "Believe," and the sinner cannot see how believing in Jesus will enable him to get the mastery over a besetting sin. There does not at first sight appear to be any connection between the simple trusting of the Savior and the conquest of a bad temper, or the getting rid of a bad habit, such as intemperance, passion, covetousness, or falsehood. There is such a connection, but recollect, whether you can see the connection or not, it is yours "not to reason why," but yours to do what Jesus bids you do, for it is in the way of the command that the miracle of mercy will be wrought. "Fill the waterpots with water,"

The Waterpots at Cana 51

though what you want is wine. Christ sees a connection between the water and the wine though you do not. He has a reason for the pots being filled with water, which reason, as yet, you do not know. It is not yours to ask an explanation, but to yield obedience. You are, in the first instance, just to do what Jesus bids you, as He bids you, now that He bids you, and because He bids you, and you shall find that His commandments are not grievous, and in keeping of them there is a great reward.

Sometimes these commands may even seem to be trivial. They may look as if He trifled with us. The family was in need of wine; Jesus says, "Fill the waterpots with water." The servants might have said, "This is clearly a mere putting of us off and playing with us. Why, we would be better employed in going around to these poor people's friends, asking them to contribute another skin of wine. We should be much better employed in finding out some shop where we could purchase more; but to send us to the well to fill those great waterpots that hold so much water does seem altogether a piece of child's play." I know, friends, that sometimes the path of duty seems as if it could not lead to the desired result. We want to be doing something more; that something more might be wrong, but it looks as if we could thereby compass our design more easily and directly, and so we hanker after this uncommanded and perhaps forbidden course. And I know that many a troubled conscience thinks that simply to believe in Jesus is too little a thing. The deceitful heart suggests a course which looks to be more effectual. "Do some penance; feel some bitterness; weep a certain amount of tears. Goad your mind, or break your heart": so cries carnal self. Jesus simply commands, "Believe." It does appear to be too little a thing to be done, as if it could not be that eternal life should be given upon putting your trust in Jesus Christ. But this is the principle we want to teach you—that when Jesus Christ is about to give a blessing He issues a command which is not to be questioned but to be at once obeyed. If you will not believe, neither shall you be established; but if you are willing and obedient, you shall eat the good of the land. "Whatsoever he saith unto you, do it."

The third principle is this—that *whenever we get a command from Christ it is always wise to carry it out zealously.* He said, "Fill the waterpots with water," and they filled them *up to the brim.* You know there is a way of filling a waterpot, and there is another way of filling it. It is full, and you cannot heap it up; but still you can fill it up until it begins almost to run over. The liquid trembles as if it must surely fall in a crystal cascade. It is a filling fullness. In fulfilling Christ's commands, my dear brethren and sisters, let us go to their widest extent: let us fill them up to the brim. If it is "believe," oh, believe Him with all your might; trust Him with your whole heart. If it is "preach the Gospel," preach it in season and out of season, and preach the Gospel—the whole of it. Fill it up to the brim. Do not give the people a half Gospel. Give them a brimming-over Gospel. Fill the vessels up to the very brim. If you are to repent, ask to have a hearty and a deep repentance—full to the brim. If you are to believe, ask to have an intense, absolute, childlike dependence, that your faith may be full to the brim. If you are bidden pray, pray mightily: fill the vessel of prayer up to the brim. If you are to search the Scriptures for blessing, search them from end to end: fill the Bible-reading vessel up to the brim. Christ's commands are never meant to be done in a halfhearted manner. Let us throw our whole soul into whatever He commands us, even though, as yet, we cannot see the reason why He has set us the task. Christ's commands should be fulfilled with enthusiasm, and carried out to the extreme, if extreme be possible.

The fourth principle is that *our earnest action in obedience to Christ is not contrary to our dependence upon Him, but it is necessary to our dependence upon Him.* I will show you that in a moment. There are some brethren I know who say, "Hem! you hold what you call revival services, and you try to arouse people by earnest appeals and exciting addresses. Do you not see that God will do His own work? These efforts are just your trying to take the work out of God's hands. The proper way is to trust in Him, and do nothing." All right, friend. We have your word for it—that you trust in Him and do nothing. I take the liberty not to be so very certain that you do trust Him, for if I remember who you are, and I think I have been to your house, you are about the most miserable, desponding, unbelieving person that I know. You do not even know whether you are saved yourself nine times out of ten. Well now, I think you should hardly come and cry yourself up for your faith. If you had such a wonderfully great faith, there is no doubt whatever that according to your faith it would be to you. How many have been added to your church through your doing nothing this year—that blessed church of yours, where you exercise this blessed faith without works? How many have been brought in? "Well, we do not have very many additions." No, and I think you are not likely to have. If you go about the extension of the Redeemer's kingdom by inaction, I do not think that you go *the way* to work which Jesus Christ approves of. But we venture to say to you that we who go in for working for Christ with all our hearts and souls, using any means within our reach to bring men in to hear the Gospel, feel as much as ever you do that we cannot do anything at all in the matter apart from the Holy Spirit, and we trust in God, I think, almost as much as you do, because our faith has produced rather more results than yours has done. I should not wonder if it turns out that your faith without works is dead, being alone, and that our faith having works with it has been living faith after all.

The Waterpots at Cana

I will put the case thus: Jesus Christ says, "Fill the waterpots with water." The orthodox servant says, "My Lord, I fully believe that You can make wine for these people without any water, and by Your leave I will bring no water. I am not going to interfere with the work of God. I am quite certain that You do not want our help, gracious Lord. You can make these waterpots to be full of wine without our bringing a single bucket of water, and so we will not rob You of the glory of it. We will just stand back and wait for You. When the wine is made we will drink some of it and bless Your name; but meanwhile we pray You have us excused, for pails are heavy carrying, and a good many must be brought to fill all those waterpots. It would be interfering with the divine work, and so we would rather take our ease." Do you not think that servants who talked so would prove that they had no faith in Jesus at all? We will not say that it would prove their unbelief, but we will say that it looks very like it. But look at the servant there who, as soon as ever Jesus commands "Fill the waterpots with water," says, "I do not know what He is at. I do not see the connection between fetching this water and providing the feast with wine, but I am off to the well. Here, hand me a couple of pails. Come along, friend; come along and help fill the baths." There they go and soon come joyfully back with the water, pouring it into the troughs until they are full up to the brim. Those seem to me to be the believing servants who obey the command, not understanding it, but expecting that, somehow or other, Jesus Christ knows the way to work His own miracle. By our earnest exertions we are not interfering with Him, dear friends; far from it. We are proving our faith in Him if we work for Him as He bids us work, and trust in Him alone with undivided faith.

The next principle I must lay equal stress upon is this—*our action alone is not sufficient*. That we know, but let me remind you of it yet again. There are these waterpots, these troughs, these baths. They are full and could not be fuller. What a spilling of water there is! You see that in their trying to fill them the water runs over here and there. Well, all these six great baths are full of water. Is there any more wine for all that? Not a drop. It is water that they brought, nothing but water, and it remains water still. Suppose that they should take that water into the feast I am half afraid that the guests would not have thought cold water quite the proper liquid to drink at a wedding. They ought to have done so; but I am afraid they were not educated in the school of total abstinence. They would have said to the master of the feast, "Thou hast given us good wine, and water is a poor finish for the feast." I am sure it would not have done. And yet water it was, depend upon it, and nothing else but water, when the servants poured it into the pots. Even so, after all that sinners can do, and all that saints can do, there is nothing in any human effort which can avail for the saving of a soul until Christ speaks the word of power. When Paul has planted and Apollos watered, there is no increase until God gives it. Preach the Gospel, labor with souls, persuade, entreat, exhort; but there is no power in anything that you do until Jesus Christ displays His divine might. His presence is our power. Blessed be His name, He will come; and if we fill the waterpots with water, He will turn it into wine. He alone can do it, and these servants who show the most alacrity in filling up the waterpots are among the first to confess that it is He alone who can perform the deed.

And now the last principle here is that *although human action in itself falls short of the desired end, yet it has its place, and God has made it necessary by His appointment.* Why did our Lord have these waterpots filled with water? I do not say that it was necessary that it should have been done. It was not absolutely necessary in itself; but in order that the miracle might be all open and aboveboard, it was necessary; for suppose He had said, "Go to those waterpots and draw out wine," those who watched Him might have said that there was wine there before, and that no miracle was wrought. When our Lord had them filled up with water, there remained no room for any wine to be hidden away. It was just the same as with Elijah, when, in order to prove that there was no concealed fire upon the altar at Carmel, he bade them go down to the sea, and bring water, and pour it upon the altar, and upon the offering, until the trenches were filled. He said, "Do it a second time," and they did it a second time; and he said, "Do it a third time," and they did it a third time, and no possibility of imposture remained. And so, when the Lord Jesus bade the servants fill the waterpots with water, He put it beyond all possibility that He should be charged with imposture; and thus we see why it was necessary that they should be filled with water.

Moreover, it was necessary, because it was so instructive to the servants. Did you notice when I was reading it that the master of the feast, when he tasted the good wine, did not know where it came from. He could not make it out, and he uttered an expression which showed his surprise, mingled with his ignorance. But it is written, "The servants which drew the water knew." Now, when souls are converted in a church, it happens much in the same way with certain of the members, who are good people, but they do not know much about the conversion of sinners. They do not feel much joy in revivals; in fact, like the elder brother, they are rather suspicious of these wild characters being brought in. They consider themselves to be very respectable, and they would rather not have the lowest of people sitting in the pew with them. They feel awkward in coming so near them. They know little about what is going on. "But the servants which drew the water knew"; that is to say, the earnest believers who do the work and try to fill the waterpots know all about it. Jesus bade them fill the vessels with water on purpose that the people who drew the water might know that it was a miracle. I warrant you, if you bring souls to Christ you will know His power. It will make you leap for joy to hear the cry of the penitent, and mark the bright flash of delight that passes over the newborn believer's face when his sins are washed away, and he feels himself renewed. If you want to know Jesus Christ's miraculous power you must go and—not work miracles, but just draw the water and fill the waterpots. Do the ordinary duties of Christian men and women—things in which there is no power of themselves, but which Jesus Christ makes to be connected with His divine working, and it shall be for your instruction, and your comfort, that you had such work to do. "The servants which drew the water knew."

I think that I have said enough upon the principles which He concealed within my text.

How to Carry Out This Divine Command

First, *use in the service of Christ such abilities as you have*. There stood the waterpots, six of them, and Jesus used what He found ready to His hand. There was water in the well; our Lord used that also. Our Lord is accustomed to employ His own people and such abilities as they have, rather than angels or a novel class of beings created fresh for the purpose. Now, dear brothers and sisters, if you have no golden chalices, fill your earthen vessels. If you cannot consider yourselves to be goblets of rarest workmanship in silver, or if you could not liken yourselves to the best Sèvres ware, it does not matter; fill the vessels which you have. If you cannot, with Elias, bring fire from heaven, and if you cannot work miracles with the apostles, do what you can. If silver and gold you have none, yet such as you have dedicate to Christ. Bring water at His bidding, and it will be better than wine. The most common gifts can be made to serve Christ's purpose. Just as He took a few loaves and fishes and fed the crowd with them, so will He take your six waterpots and the water, and do His wine-making therewith.

Thus, you see, they improved what they had; for the waterpots were empty, but they filled them. There are a good many brethren here from the College tonight, and they are trying to improve their gifts and their abilities. I think you do right, my brethren. But I have heard some people say, "The Lord Jesus does not want your learning." No, it is very likely that He does not any more than He needed the water. But then He certainly does not want your stupidity and your ignorance, and He does not want your rough, uncultivated ways of speaking. He did not seek for empty pitchers on this occasion; He would have them full, and the servants did well to fill them. Our Lord today does not want empty

GOD DOESN'T WANT US AS EMPTY VESSELS

heads in His ministers, nor empty hearts; so, my brethren, fill your waterpots with water. Work away, and study away, and learn all you can, and fill the waterpots with water. "Oh," somebody will say, "but how are such studies to lead to the conversion of people? Conversion is like wine, and all that these young fellows will learn will be like water." You are right; but still I bid these students fill the waterpots with water, and expect the Lord Jesus to turn the water into wine. He can sanctify human knowledge so that it shall be useful to the setting forth of the knowledge of Jesus Christ. I hope that the day has gone by when it is so much as dreamed that ignorance and coarseness are helpful to the kingdom of Christ. The great Teacher would have His people know all that they can know, and especially know Him, and the Scriptures, that they may set Him forth, and proclaim His Gospel. "Fill the waterpots with water."

Next, to apply this principle, let us all *use such means of blessing as God appoints.* What are they? First, there is the reading of the Scriptures. "Search the Scriptures." Search them all you can. Try to understand them. "But if I know the Bible, shall I be therefore saved?" No, you must know Christ Himself by the Spirit. Still, "fill the waterpots with water." While you are studying the Scriptures you may expect the Savior will bless His own Word, and turn the water into wine.

Then there is attendance upon the means of grace and hearing a Gospel ministry. Mind you fill that waterpot with water. "But I may hear thousands of sermons and not be saved." I know it is so, but your business is to fill this waterpot with water, and while you are listening to the Gospel God will bless it, for "faith cometh by hearing, and hearing by the word of God." Take care to use the means which God appoints. Since our Lord has appointed to save men and women by the preaching of the Word, I pray that He will raise up those who will preach without ceasing, in season and out of season, indoors and in the streets. "But they won't be saved by our preaching." I know that. Preaching is the water; and while we are preaching, God will bless it, and turn the water into wine. Let us distribute religious books and tracts. "Oh, but people won't be saved by reading them." Very likely not, but while they are reading them God may bring His truth to remembrance and impress their hearts. "Fill the waterpots with water." Give away abundance of tracts. Scatter religious literature everywhere. "Fill the waterpots with water," and the Lord will turn the water into wine.

Remember the prayer meeting. What a blessed means of grace it is, for it brings down power for all the works of the church: fill that waterpot with water. I have no complaint of your attendance at prayer meetings; but oh, keep it up, dear ones! You can pray. Blessed be His name, you have the spirit of prayer. Pray on! "Fill the waterpots with water,"

The Waterpots at Cana

and in answer to prayer Jesus will turn it into wine. Sunday school teachers, do not neglect your blessed means of usefulness. "Fill the waterpots with water." Work the Sunday school system with all your might. "But it will not save the children merely to get them together and teach them of Jesus. We cannot give them new hearts." Who said that you could? "Fill the waterpots with water." Jesus Christ knows how to turn it into wine, and He does not fail to do it when we are obedient to His commands.

Use all the means, but *take care that you use those mean's right heartily*. I come back to that part of the text—"And they filled them up to the brim." When you teach the young ones in the Sunday school, teach them well. Fill them to the brim. When you preach, dear sir, do not preach as if you were only half awake; stir yourself up; fill your ministry to the brim. When you are trying to evangelize the community, do not attempt it in a halfhearted way, as if you did not care whether their souls were saved or not; fill them to the brim; preach the Gospel with all your might, and beg for power from on high. Fill every vessel to the brim. Whatever is worth doing is worth doing well. Nobody ever yet served Christ too well. I have heard that in some services there may be too much zeal, but in the service of Christ you may have as much zeal as ever you will and yet not exceed, if prudence be joined therewith. "Fill the waterpots with water," and fill them to the brim. Go in for doing good with all your heart and soul and strength.

Further, in order to apply this principle, be sure to *remember when you have done all that you can do, that there is a great deficiency in all that you have done*. It is well to come away from tract distributing and Sunday school teaching and preaching, and go home and get to your knees, and cry, "Lord, I have done all that You have commanded me, and yet there is nothing done unless You give the finishing touch. Lord, I have filled the waterpots, and though I could only fill them with water, yet I have filled them to the brim. Lord, to the best of my ability, I have sought to win people for Yourself. There cannot be a soul saved, a child converted, or any glory brought to Your name by what I have done in and of itself; but, my Master, speak the miracle working word, and let the water which fills the vessels blush into wine. You can do it, though I cannot. I cast the burden upon You."

And this leads me to the last application of the principle, which is—*trust in your Lord to do the work*. You see, there are two ways of filling waterpots. Suppose these people had never been commanded to fill the waterpots, and their doing it had had no reference to Christ whatever. Suppose that it had been a freak of their own imagination, and they had said, "These people have no wine, but they shall have a bath if they like, and so we will fill the six waterpots with water." Nothing would have come of such a proceeding. There would have stood the water. The Eton school boy said, "The conscious water saw its God and blushed," a truly poetic expression; but the conscious water would have seen the servants and would not have blushed. It would have reflected their faces upon its shining surface, but nothing more would have happened. Jesus Christ Himself must come and in present power must work the miracle. It was because He had commanded the servants to fill the waterpots with water that therefore He was bound, if I may use such an expression of our free King, bound to turn it into wine, for otherwise He would have been making fools of them, and they also might have turned around and said, "Why did You give us such a command as this?" If, after we have filled the waterpots with water, Jesus does not work by us, we shall have done what He bade us. But if we believe in Him, I make bold to say that He is bound to come. For though we would be losers, and dreadful losers too, if He did not display His power, for we would have to lament, "I have labored in vain, and spent my strength for nothing," yet we would not be such losers as He would be, for straightway the world would affirm that Christ's commands are empty, fruitless, idle. It would be declared that obedience to His Word brings no result. The world would say, "You have filled the waterpots with water because He told you to do it. You expected Him to turn the water into wine, but He did not do it. Your faith is vain; your whole obedience is vain; He is not a fit Master to be served." *We* would be losers, but *He* would be a greater loser still, for He would lose His glory.

For my part, I do not believe that a good word for Christ is ever spoken in vain. I am sure that no sermon with Christ in it is ever preached without result. Something will come of it, if not tonight, nor tomorrow; something will come of it. When I have printed a sermon, and seen it fairly in the volume, I have before long been delighted to hear of souls saved by its means. And when I have not printed, but only preached a discourse, I have still thought, something will come of it. I preached Christ. I put His saving truth into that sermon and that seed cannot die. If it shall lie in the volume for years, like the grains of wheat in the mummy's hand, it will live, and grow, and bear fruit. Consequently, I have heard but lately of a soul brought to Christ by a sermon that I preached twenty-five years ago. I hear almost every week of souls having been brought to Christ by sermons preached at Park Street, and Exeter Hall, and the Surrey Gardens, and therefore I feel that God will not let a single faithful testimony fall to the ground. Go on, brothers and sisters. Go on filling the waterpots with water. Do not believe that you are doing much when you have done your utmost. Do not begin to congratulate yourselves on your past success. All must come from Christ; and it *will* come from Christ. Do not go to the prayer meeting and say, "Paul *may* plant and Apollos *may* water, but"—and so on. That is not how the passage runs. It says just the contrary, and runs thus—"Paul planteth, Apollos watereth, but God giveth the increase." The increase is surely given by God where the planting and sowing are rightly done. The servants fill the waterpots; the Master turns the water into wine.

The Lord grant us grace to be obedient to His command, especially to that command, "Believe and live!" And may we meet Him in the marriage feast above to drink of the new wine with Him forever and ever. Amen and amen.

5
An Astounding Miracle

And they went into Capernaum; and straightway on the sabbath day he entered into the synagogue, and taught. And they were astonished at his doctrine: for he taught them as one that had authority and not as the scribes. And there was in their synagogue a man with an unclean spirit; and he cried out, saying, Let us alone; what have we to do with thee, thou Jesus of Nazareth? art thou come to destroy us? I know thee who thou art, the Holy One of God. And Jesus rebuked him, saying, Hold thy peace, and come out of him. And when the unclean spirit had torn him, and cried with a loud voice, he came out of him. And they were all amazed, insomuch that they questioned among themselves, saying, What thing is this? what new doctrine is this? for with authority commandeth he even the unclean spirits, and they do obey him. And immediately his fame spread abroad throughout all the region round about Galilee (Mark 1:21–28).

You will find the same narrative in Luke 4:31–37. It will be handy for you to be able to refer to the second passage, from which I shall quote one or two matters.

These two Evangelists commence the narrative by telling us of the singular authority and power which there was about the Savior's teaching—authority, so that no one dare question His doctrine; power, so that everyone felt the force of the truth which He delivered. "They were astonished at his teaching, for his word was with power." Why was it that the Savior's teaching had such a remarkable power about it? Was it not, first, because He preached the truth? There is no power in falsehood except so far as people choose to yield to it because it flatters them; but there is great force in truth, it makes its own way into the soul. As long as people have consciences they cannot help feeling

---

This sermon was taken from *The Metropolitan Tabernacle Pulpit* and was preached on Sunday morning, February 10, 1884.

An Astounding Miracle

when the truth is brought to bear upon them. Even though they grow angry their very resistance proves that they recognize the force of what is spoken. Moreover, the Savior spoke the truth in a very natural, unaffected manner: the truth was in Him, and it flowed freely from Him. His manner was truthful as well as His matter. There is a way of speaking truth so as to make it sound like a lie. Perhaps there is no greater injury done to truth than when it is spoken in a doubtful manner, with none of the accent and emphasis of conviction. Our Savior spoke as the oracles of God. He spoke truth as truth should be spoken, unaffectedly and naturally, as one who did not preach professionally, but out of the fullness of His heart. You all know how sermons from the heart go to the heart. Moreover, our great Exemplar delivered His teaching as one who most heartily believed what He was speaking, who spoke what He did know, yes, spoke of things which were His own. Jesus had no doubts, no hesitancy, no questions, and His style was as calmly forcible as His faith. Truth seemed to be reflected from His face just as it shone forth from God in all its native purity and splendor. He could not speak otherwise than He did, for He spoke as He was, as He felt, and as He knew. Our Lord spoke as one whose life supported all that He taught. Those who knew Him could not say, "He speaks after a right kind, but He acts otherwise." There was about His whole conduct and deportment that which made Him the fit person to utter the truth, because the truth was incarnate, and embodied, and exemplified in His own person. Well might He speak with great assurance when He could say, "Which of you convinceth me of sin?" He was Himself as pure as the truth which He proclaimed. He was not a speaking machine, sounding out something with which it has no vital connection; but out of the midst of His own heart there flowed rivers of living waters. Truth overflowed at His lips from the deep well of His soul; it was in Him and therefore came from Him. What He poured forth was His own life, wherewith He was endeavoring to impregnate the lives of others. Consequently, for all these reasons, and many besides, Jesus spoke as one that had authority: His tone was commanding, His teaching was convincing.

Meanwhile, the Holy Spirit, who had descended upon Him in His baptism, rested upon Him and bore witness by His divine operations in the consciences and hearts of men and women. If Jesus spoke of sin, the Spirit was there to convince the world of sin. If He set forth a glorious righteousness, the Holy Spirit was there to convince the world of righteousness; and when He told people of the coming judgment, the Holy Spirit was present to make them know that a judgment would surely come at which each of them must appear. Because of His unlimited anointing by the Spirit, our Lord spoke with power and authority of the most astonishing kind, so that all who heard Him were compelled to feel that no ordinary Rabbi stood before them.

That power and authority was seen all the more in contrast with the scribes, for the scribes spoke hesitatingly. They quoted authority. They begged leave to venture an opinion. They supported their ideas by the opinion of Rabbi This, although it was questioned by Rabbi The Other. They spent their time in tying and untying knots before the people, quibbling about matters which had no practical importance whatever. They were wonderfully clear upon the tithing of mint and anise; they enlarged most copiously upon the washing of cups and basins; they were profound upon phylacteries and borders of garments. They were at home upon such rubbish, which would neither save a soul, nor slay a sin, nor suggest a virtue. While handling the Scriptures they were mere word-triflers, letter-men, whose chief object was to show their own wisdom. Such attempts at oratory and word spinning were as far as the poles asunder from the discourses of our Lord. Self-display never entered into the mind of Jesus. He Himself was so absorbed in what He had to teach that His hearers did not exclaim, "What a preacher is this!" but, "What a word is this! "and "What new teaching is this!" The word and the teaching with their admirable authority and amazing power subduing people's minds and hearts by the energy of truth. People acknowledged that the great teacher had taught them something worth knowing, and had so impressed it upon them that there was no shaking themselves free of it.

Now, when they were beginning to perceive this authority in His word, our Lord determined to prove to them that there was real power at the back of His teaching, that He had a right to use such authority, for He was Jesus Christ the Son of God, clothed with divine authority and power. It occurred to Him to display before their eyes the fact that as there was power about His speech, there was also power about Himself, that He was mighty in deed as well as in word; hence He wrought the miracle now before us. This most astounding deed of authority and power has been passed over by certain expositors as having too little of incident about it to be of much interest, whereas, to my mind, it rises in some respects above all other miracles, and is certainly excelled by none in its forcible demonstration of our Lord's authority and power. It is the first miracle which Mark gives us; it is the first which Luke gives us; and it is in some respects the first of miracles, as I hope I may show before I have done. Remember, however, that the object of the miracle is to reveal more fully the power and authority of our Lord's word, and to let us see by signs following that His teaching has an omnipotent force about it. This truth is much needed at the present moment; for if the Gospel does not still save people, if it is not still "the power of God

An Astounding Miracle

unto salvation to every one that believeth," then the attacks of skepticism are not easily repelled. But if it is still a thing of power over the minds of men and women, a power conquering sin and Satan, then they may say what they like, our only answer shall be to lament their doubts and to scorn their scorning. O for an hour of the Son of Man! O where is He that trod the sea and bade the rage of hell subside with a word?

The Beneficiary of the Miracle

This person was, first, *one possessed*. A devil dwelt within him. We cannot explain this fact any more than we can explain madness. Many things which happen in the world of mind are quite inexplicable, and for the matter of that so are many facts in the world of matter. We accept the recorded fact—an evil spirit entered into this man, and continued in him. Satan, you know, is God's ape; he is always trying to imitate Him, to caricature Him; so, when God became incarnate, it occurred to Satan to become incarnate too. This man I may call, without any misuse of words, an incarnate devil; or, at any rate, the devil was incarnated in him. He had become like a devil in human form, and so was in a certain manner the opposite of our Lord Jesus. In Jesus dwelt the fullness of the Godhead bodily by an eternal union; in this man the devil dwelt for a while. Is not this an awful picture? But note the fact, the man whom Jesus selects on whom to prove His power and authority was so far gone that the foul fiend controlled his mind, and made a kennel of his body. I wondered, when thinking this over, whether a person of whom this man is the emblem would come into the congregation today, for I have seen such people. I have not dared personally to apply such an epithet to anyone, but I have heard it applied. I have heard disgusted friends and indignant neighbors, worn out with the drunken profanity, or horrible filthiness, of some man say, "He does not seem to be human; he acts like the Evil One." Or when it has been a woman, they have said, "All that is womanly is gone; she seems to be a female fiend." Well, if such shall come within sound of my voice or within leading of this sermon, let them take note that there is help, hope, and health even for them. The power of Jesus knows no limit. Upon one who was the Devil's own did our gracious Lord display His authority and power in connection with His Gospel teaching; He is not less able now than then.

This man, further, was *one whose personality was to a great extent merged in the Evil One*. Read the twenty-third verse: "There was in their synagogue a man with an unclean spirit"; the rendering might be equally accurate if we read it, "A man in an unclean spirit." See you that? Not only a man *with* an unclean spirit in him, but a man *in* an unclean spirit. The phrase is simple enough; we speak of a man being in drink. For liquor to be in a man does not mean half so much as for a man to be in liquor. To give a more pleasant illustration, we speak of a person's being "in love"; he is absorbed in his affection. We should not express a tenth as much if we said that love is in the man. A man can be in a rage, in a passion; and even so was this man in an evil spirit. He was completely ruled of the Evil One. The poor creature had no power over himself whatever, and was not himself actually responsible; in all that I say of him I am not condemning *him*, but only using him as a type of human sin. Please do not forget this. As far as the narrative is concerned the man himself scarcely appears; it is the unclean spirit that cries out, "Let us alone; I know thee who thou art." These are words spoken by the man, but they are the sentiments of the demon who used the man's organs of speech according to his own will. The man was scarcely a man with a will or wish of his own; in fact, you do not notice him until you see him flung down into the midst of the synagogue; you only see the proper man when the Savior raises him before them all, unharmed and rational. Until the miracle is wrought the man is lost in the unclean sprit that dominates him. Have you never seen such people? You say sometimes, and you say truly, "Alas, poor wretch! The drink has the mastery over him; he would never do such things as he does if he was not in drink." We do not mean to excuse him by such an expression, far from it. Or it may be the man is a gambler, and you say, "He is quite besotted by gaming though he impoverishes his wife and children, yet he is possessed by that spirit so completely that he has not the mind nor the will to resist the temptation." Or it may be that such another person is carried away with unchaste affections, and we say, "How sad! There was something about that man which we used to like; in many points he was admirable, but he is so deluded by his bad passions that he does not seem to be himself." We almost forget the person, and think mainly of the dreadful spirit which has degraded him or her below the beasts. The type and emblem of such a person as this our Lord selected as the platform whereon to show His power. I wonder whether this voice of mine will reach one of that sort. I sincerely hope that none of you are in such a condition; but if you should be, still there is hope for you in Christ Jesus. He is able to deliver such as are led captive at the will of Satan. Though you seem wholly given up and utterly abandoned to the dominion of a terrible sin to which you yield a willing obedience, yet Jesus can break off the iron yoke from your neck and bring you into the liberty of holiness. It will be an awful thing for you to die in your sins, and you surely will unless you believe in the Lord Jesus. But if you look to Him, He can make you pure and holy, and create you anew.

Note further, for we must show you how our Lord selects the worst of cases, it was a man *in whom the evil spirit was at his worst.* Kindly

An Astounding Miracle

look at the fourth chapter of Luke, verse thirty-three, and you will see that in this man there was "the spirit of an unclean devil." Think of that. A devil is never particularly clean at any time; what must an unclean devil be? The ruling spirit in the man was not only a devil, but an *unclean* devil. Satan sometimes cleans himself up, and comes out quite bright and shining, like an angel of light; but do not mistake him; he is still a devil, for all his pretended purity. There are glittering sins, and respectable sins, and these will ruin souls; but this poor man had a disreputable demon in him, a spirit of the foulest, coarsest, and most abominable order. I suppose this foul spirit would incite its victim to filthy talk and obscene acts. The evil one delights in sins against the seventh commandment. If he can lead men and women to defile their bodies he takes special delight in such crimes. I doubt not that this poor creature was reduced to the most brutal form of animalism. I can well believe that in his body he was filthy, and that in his talk, in all the thoughts that hurried through his poor brain, and in all his actions, he went to a pitch of uncleanness upon which we need not permit a conjecture. If we were to say of such a character as this man pictures, "Let us turn out of the way," who could blame us? If we separated from such sinners, who could censure us? We do not desire to go near to Satan in any shape, but most of all we would shun him when he is openly and avowedly unclean. You say, "We could not bear to hear the man speak; the very look of him is offensive," nor is it strange that you should. There are women so fallen that modesty trembles to be seen in their company, and the feeling that makes you shudder at them is not to be condemned, so long as it does not spring from self-righteousness or lead to contempt. Yet, now, see it and wonder, our blessed Lord and Master fixed His eye of old on the man with the unclean devil in him, and today He fixes His eye of mercy on the basest and vilest of mankind, that in their conversion He may show the power and authority of His word. Lord, do so at this moment. Let us see today the miracles of Your grace. Bring the chief of sinners to repentance! Upraise those who are fallen the lowest!

In this man there did not seem to be anything for the Lord to begin upon. When you are trying to bring someone to the Savior you look over him to see where you can touch him, what there is in him that you can work upon. Perhaps he is a good husband though he is a drunkard, and you wisely attempt to work upon his domestic affections. If a person has some point of character upon which you can rest your lever, your work is comparatively easy. But with some people you look over them from top to bottom, and you cannot find a spot for hope to rest upon. They seem so utterly gone that there is neither reason, nor conscience, nor will, nor power of thought left in them. Of all this the possessed man in the synagogue is a striking emblem, for when the Lord comes into the synagogue the poor wretch does not begin to pray, "Lord, heal me." No, his first cry is, "Let us alone." He does not seem to resist this cry of the evil spirit in him though it was so much to his own injury, but he goes on to say, "What have we to do with thee, thou Jesus of Nazareth? Art thou come to destroy us? I know thee who thou art." The possessed man seems wholly lost in the dominating spirit of evil which permeates his entire being. Now I look upon this, though it be negative, as a very glaring part of the difficulty. For I do not care how far a person has gone in outward sin, if he has some point left in him of common honesty, or love to his family, or generous heartedness, you know where to commence operations, and your work is hopeful. Even leviathan has some crevice between his scales though they be shut up together as with a close seal. There is some joint in the harness of most people, even though sin may cover them from head to foot; but in those outcasts of whom I am now speaking there is neither lodgment for hope, nor foothold for faith, nor more than a bare ledge for love. As the man in the synagogue was shut up within the demon's influence, so are some people encompassed by their iniquity, blocked up by their depravity. Yet the great Upraiser of the fallen can rescue even these; He is able to save to the uttermost.

One other matter makes the case still more terrible: *he was a man upon whom religious observances were lost.* He was in the synagogue on the Sabbath, and I do not suppose that this was anything unusual. The worst person of all is one who can attend the means of grace, and yet remain under the full power of evil. Those poor outside sinners who know nothing of the Gospel at all, and never go to the house of God at all, for them there remains at least the hope that the very novelty of the Holy Word may strike them but as for those who are continually in our synagogues, what shall now be done for them if they remain in sin? It is singular, but true, that Satan will come to a place of worship. "Oh," say you, "surely he will never do that?" He did it so long back as the days of Job, when the sons of God came to present themselves before the Lord, and Satan came also amongst them. The evil spirit led this unhappy man to the synagogue that morning, and it may be he did so with the idea of disturbing the teaching of the Lord Jesus Christ. I am glad he was there. I wish that all the slaves of sin and Satan would attend upon Sabbath worship. They are then within range of the Gospel, and who can tell how many may be reached? Yet how sad it was that the influences of religious worship had altogether failed to rescue this man from his thralldom! They sang in the synagogue, but they could not sing the evil spirit out of him. They read the lessons of the day in the synagogue, but they could not read the foul spirit out of him. They gave addresses from passages of Scripture, but they could not address the

An Astounding Miracle

unclean spirit out of him. No doubt some of the godly prayed for him, but they could not pray the devil out of him. Nothing can cast out Satan but the word of Jesus Himself. His own word, from His own lip, has power and authority about it, but everything short of that falls to the ground. O Divine Redeemer, let Your omnipotence be displayed in turning great sinners into sincere penitents!

You see, then, what a terrible case the Master selected. I have not exaggerated, I am sure. O the comfort which lies in the thought that he still chooses to save persons of whom this wretched being is the fit emblem and representative! O you vilest of the vile, here is hope for you!

The Enemy of the Miracle

Our Lord encounters a firmly-entrenched enemy. The evil spirit in this man had ramparted and bulwarked himself against the assault of Christ, for as I have said, *he had the man fully at his command*, he could make him say and do whatever be pleased. He had that man so at his command that he brought him to the synagogue that day and *he compelled him to become a disturber of the worship*. Quietness and order should be in the assemblies of God's people, but this poor soul was egged on to cry out and make horrible noises so as to raise great tumult in the congregation. The Jews allowed all the liberty they could to persons possessed, and so long as their behavior was bearable they were tolerated in the synagogues; but this poor mortal broke through the bounds of propriety, and his cries were a terror to all. But see, the Lord Jesus deals with this disturber; this is the very man in whom He will be glorified. So have I seen my Lord convert His most furious enemy, and enlist to His service the most violent of opposers.

The Evil One *compelled his victim to beg to be left alone*: as we have it here, "Let us alone." In the Revised Version of Luke the same rendering is put in the margin, but in the text we have "Ah!" While the Lord Jesus was teaching there was suddenly heard a terrible "Ah!" A horrible, hideous outcry startled all, and these words were heard: "Ah! what have we to do with thee?" It was not the voice of supplication; it was distinctly the reverse; it was a prayer not *for* mercy, but *against* mercy. The translation is however quite good if we read, "Let us alone." Is it not a horrible thing that Satan leads people to say, "Do not trouble us with your Gospel! Do not bother us with religion! Do not come here with your tracts! Let us alone!" They claim the wretched right to perish in their sins, the liberty to destroy their own souls. We know who rules when they speak thus. It is the prince of darkness who makes them hate the light. Oh, my hearers, do not some of you say, "We do not want to be worried with thoughts of death, and judgment, and eternity. We do not desire to hear about repentance and faith in a Savior; all we want of religious people is that they will let us alone." This cruel kindness we cannot grant them. How can we stand by and see them perish? Yet how sad the moral condition of one who does not wish to be made pure! You would think it impossible for Jesus to do anything with a man while he is crying out, "Let us alone"; yet it was the evil spirit in this man that our Lord met and overcame. Is there not encouragement for us to deal with those who give us no welcome, but shut the door in our faces?

The foul spirit *made the man renounce all interest in Christ*. He coupled him with himself, and made him say, "What have we to do with thee, thou Jesus of Nazareth?" This was a disclaimer of all connection with the Savior. He almost resented the Savior's presence as an intrusion. The voice seems to cry to Jesus, "I have nothing to do with You; go Your way and leave me alone. I do not want You; whatever You can do to save or bless me is hereby refused. Only let me alone." Now, when a person deliberately says, "I will have nothing to do with your Jesus. I want no pardon, no salvation, no heaven," I think the most of you would say, "That is a hopeless case; we had better go elsewhere." Yet even when Satan has led someone this length the Lord can drive him out. He is mighty to save. He can change even the hardest heart.

The unclean spirit did more than that: *he caused this man to dread the Savior*, and made him cry out, "Ah! Art thou come to destroy us?" Many persons are afraid of the Gospel; to them religion wears a gloomy aspect. They do not care to hear of it for fear it would make them melancholy and rob them of their pleasures. "Oh," say they, "religion would get me into Bedlam; it would drive me mad." Thus Satan by his detestable falsehoods makes people dread their best friend, and tremble at that which would make them happy forever.

A further entrenchment Satan had cast up: *he made his victim yield an outward assent to the Gospel*. "I know thee who thou art," said the spirit, speaking with the man's lips, "the Holy One of God." Of all forms of Satan's devices this is one of the worst for workers, when people say, "Yes, yes, what you say is very proper!" You call upon them and talk about Jesus, and they answer, "Yes, sir. It is quite true. I am much obliged to you, sir." You preach the Gospel, and they say, "He made an interesting discourse, and he is a very clever man!" You buttonhole them, and speak about the Savior, and they reply, "It is very kind of you to talk to me so earnestly; I always admire this sort of thing. Zeal is much to be commended in these days." This is one of the strongest of earthworks, for the cannonballs sink into it, and their force is gone. This makes Satan secure in his hold on the heart. Yet the Savior dislodged this demon, and therein displayed His power and authority.

An Astounding Miracle

Have I not proved my point? Jesus selected a most unhappy individual to become an instance of His supremacy over the powers of darkness. He selected a most firmly entrenched spirit to be chased out of the nature which had become his stronghold.

The Manner of the Miracle

Our Lord conquered in a most signal manner. The conquest *began as soon as the Savior entered the synagogue*, and was thus under the same roof with the devil. Then the Evil One began to fear. That first cry of "Ah," or "Let us alone," shows that the evil spirit knew his Conqueror. Jesus had not said anything to the man. No, but the presence of Christ and His teaching are the terror of fiends. Wherever Jesus Christ comes in Satan knows that he must go out. Jesus has come to destroy the works of the Devil, and the Evil One is aware of his fate. Now, as soon as ever one of you shall go into a house with the desire to bring the inmates to Christ it will be telegraphed to the bottomless pit directly. Insignificant person as you may think yourself, you are a very dangerous person to Satan's kingdom if you go in the name of Jesus and tell out His Gospel. The Lord Jesus Christ opened the book and read in the synagogue, and soon His explanation and His teaching with authority and power made all the evil spirits feel that their kingdom was shaken. "I beheld," said our Lord at another time, "Satan fall like lightning from heaven"; and that fall was commencing in this "beginning of the gospel of Jesus Christ the Son of God." The first token of our Lord's triumph was the evident alarm which caused the evil spirit to cry out.

The next sign was *that the devil began to offer terms to Christ*, for I take it that is the reason why he said, "I know thee who thou art, the Holy One of God." He did not confront our Lord with the hostile doubt, "If You are the Son of God"; but with the complaisant compliment, "I know thee who thou art." "Yes," the false spirit said, "I will allow this man to say his creed, and avow himself one of the orthodox, and then perhaps I shall be let alone. The man is sound in his views, and so my living in him cannot be a bad thing after all. I am quite willing to admit all the claims of Jesus, so long as He will not interfere with my rule over the man." The Evil One had read his Bible, and knew how Daniel had called Jesus "the Most Holy," and so he calls him "The Holy One of God." "I am quite willing to admit it all," says the devil, "only let me stay in the man; do not meddle with me, and this man's lips shall confess the truth." And so, when Jesus comes in His power, and people hear His word, this deceitful compromise is often proposed and attempted. The sinner says, "I believe it all. I deny nothing. I am no infidel; but I mean to keep my sin; and I do not intend to feel the power of the Gospel so as to repent and have my sin chased out of me. I will agree to the Gospel, but I will not allow it to control my life." However, this coming to terms shows that the fallen spirit knows his Destroyer. He would fain be let down easily. He is willing to crouch, to cringe, to fawn, and even to bear that den a human soul. Liar as he is, it must go sadly against the grain for him to say, "I know thee who thou art"; yet he will do this if he may be allowed to keep dominion. So when Jesus draws near to human minds, they say, "We will be orthodox, we will believe the Bible, and we will do anything else you prescribe, only do not disturb our consciences, interfere with our habits, or dislodge our selfishness." People will accept anything rather than renounce their sin, their pride, their ease.

Then came our Lord's real work on this man. *He gave the evil spirit short and sharp orders.* "Silence! Come out!" "Jesus rebuked him." The word implies that He spoke sharply to him. How else could He speak to one who was maliciously tormenting a man who had done him no harm? The Greek word might be read, "Be muzzled." It is a harsh word, such as an unclean tormenting spirit deserves. "Silence! Come out." That is exactly what Jesus means that the devil shall do when He delivers people from him. He says to him, "Come out of the man; I do not want pious talk and orthodox professing; hold your peace and come out of him." It is not for evil spirits, nor yet for ungodly men and women, to try to honor Christ by their words. Traitors bring no honor to those they praise; liars cannot bear witness to the truth, for if they do they damage its cause. "Be still," says Jesus; then, "Come out." He speaks as a person might call a dog out of a kennel, "Come out." "Oh," says the unclean spirit, "let me stay, and the man shall go to church; he shall even go to the sacrament." "No," says the Lord, "Come out of him. You have no right within him; he is Mine, and not yours. Come out of him!" I pray that the Master may give one of His mighty calls at this moment, speak to some poor besotted creature, and say to the devil in him, "Come out of him!" O sinners, sin must quit you or it will ruin you forever. Are you not eager to be rid of it?

Now see the conquest of Christ ever the unclean spirit. *The fiend did not dare to utter another word*, though he went as near it as he could. He "cried with a loud voice." He made an inarticulate howling as he left the man. As he came out he tried to do his victim some further injury, but in that also he failed. He tore at him, and threw him down in the midst of the synagogue, but Luke adds, "He came out of him, having done him no hurt." From the moment when Jesus bade him "come out," his power to harm was gone; he came out like a whipped cur. See how Jesus triumphs. As he did this literally in the man in the synagogue, so he does it spiritually in thousands of cases. The last act of the fiend was malicious, but fruitless. I have seen a poor creature rolled in

An Astounding Miracle

the lust of despair by the departing Enemy, but he has soon risen to joy and peace. Have you not seen him in the inquiry room, weeping in the dismay of his spirit? But that has caused him no real harm, it has even been a benefit to him by causing him to feel a deeper sense of sin, and by driving him quite out of himself to the Savior. Oh, what a splendid triumph this is for our Lord when out of a great sinner the reigning power of sin is expelled by a word! How our Master tramples on the lion and the adder! How He treads under His feet the young lion and the dragon! If the Lord will speak with power today to any soul, however vicious, or depraved, or besotted, his reigning sins shall come out of him, and the poor sinner shall become a trophy of His sovereign grace.

The Astonishment of the Miracle

The Savior raises by what He did a great wonderment. The people that saw this were more astonished than they generally were at the Savior's miracles, for they said, "What thing is this? What new teaching is this? for with authority commandeth he even the unclean spirits, and they do obey him." The wonder lay in this: here *was a man at his very lowest*; he could not be worse. I have shown you the impossibility of anybody being worse than this poor creature was. I mean not that he was evil morally, for, as I have hinted before, the moral element does not actually enter into the man's case. But he is the instructive picture of the worst man morally; utterly and entirely possessed of Satan, and carried away to an extreme degree by the force of evil. Now, under the preaching of the Gospel the worst person that lives may be saved. While he is listening to the Gospel a power goes with it which can teach the hardest heart, subdue the proudest will, change the most perverted affections, and bring the most unwilling spirit to the feet of Jesus. I speak now what I do know, because I have seen it in scores and hundreds of cases, that the least likely persons, about whom there seemed to be nothing whatever helpful to the work of grace or preparatory for it, have nevertheless been turned from the power of Satan to God. Such have been struck down by the preaching of the Gospel, and the devil has been made to come out of them, there and then, and they have become new creatures in Christ Jesus. This creates a great wonderment, and causes great staggering among the ungodly. They cannot understand it; but they ask, "What thing is this? And what new doctrine is this?" This is a convincing sign which makes the most obdurate unbeliever question his unbelief.

Notice, in this case, that *Jesus worked entirely and altogether alone*. In most of His other miracles He required faith. In order to save there must be faith; but this miracle before us is not a parable of human experience so much as of Christ's working, and that working is not dependent upon anything in the man. When a man is commanded to stretch out his withered hand, or told to go to the pool of Siloam and wash, he does something; but in this case the man is ignored. If he does anything it is rather to resist than to assist; the devil makes him cry, "Let us alone; what have we to de with thee?" The Lord Jesus Christ here displays His sovereignty, His power, and His authority, utterly ignoring the man, consulting neither his will nor his faith, but sovereignly bidding the fiend, "Be silent and come out." The thing is done, and the man is delivered from his thralldom before he has had time to seek or pray.

The miracle seems to me to teach just this, that the power of Christ to save from sin does not lie in the person saved, it lies wholly in Jesus Himself; further, I learn that though the person to be saved be so far gone that you could scarcely expect faith of him, yet the Gospel coming to him can bring faith with itself, and do its own work, *ab initio*, from the very beginning. What if I say that the Gospel is a seed that makes its own soil! It is a spark that carries its own fuel with it; a life which can implant itself within the ribs of death, ay, between the jaws of destruction. The Eternal Spirit comes with His own light and life and creates people in Christ Jesus to the praise of the glory of His grace. Oh, the marvel of this miracle! I was never led more greatly to admire the splendor of the power of Christ to rescue human beings from sin than at this hour.

And, to conclude, I notice our Lord *did nothing but speak*. In other cases He laid His hand upon the diseased, or led them out of the city, or touched them, or applied clay, or used spittle; but in this case He does not use any instrumentality; His word is all. He says, "Hold thy peace, and come out of him"; and the unclean spirit is evicted. The word of the Lord has shaken the kingdom of darkness, and loosed the bonds of the oppressed. As when the Lord scattered the primeval darkness by the fiat, "Light be," so did Jesus give the word, and its own intrinsic power banished the messenger of darkness.

Oh, you that preach Christ, preach Him boldly! No coward lips must proclaim His invincible Gospel! Oh, you that preach Christ, never choose your place of labor; never turn your back on the worst of mankind! If the Lord should send you to the borders of perdition, go there and preach Him with full assurance that it shall not be in vain. Oh, you that would win souls, have no preference as to which they shall be; or, if you have a choice, select the very worst! Remember, my Master's Gospel is not merely for the moralist, in his respectable dwelling, but for the abandoned and fallen in the filthy dens of the outcast. The all-conquering light of the Sun of Righteousness is not for the

An Astounding Miracle

dim dawn alone, to brighten it into the full blaze of day, but it is meant for the blackest midnight that ever made a soul to shiver as in the shadow of death. The name of Jesus is high over all, in heaven, and earth, and sky, therefore let us preach it with authority and confidence; not as though it were a human invention. He has said He will be with us, and therefore nothing is impossible. The Word of the Lord Jesus cannot fall to the ground; the gates of hell cannot prevail against it. The pleasure of the Lord shall prosper in His hand. The Lord shall bruise Satan under our feet shortly.

I have gone to great lengths in this sermon because I would reach sinners who have gone to great lengths. Oh, that they would accept this message of amazing mercy! He who has come to save sinners is God, and this is the surest ground of hope for the very worst. Hear this I pray you; it is the Lord your God who speaks to you, "Look unto me, and be ye saved, all the ends of the earth: for I am God, and there is none else."

6
Impotence and Omnipotence

And a certain man was there, which had an infirmity thirty and eight years. When Jesus saw him lie, and knew that he had been now a long time in that case, he saith unto him, Wilt thou be made whole? The impotent man answered him, Sir, I have no man, when the water is troubled, to put me into the pool: but while I am coming, another steppeth down before me. Jesus saith unto him, Rise, take up thy bed, and walk. And immediately the man was made whole, and took up his bed, and walked (John 5:5–9).

This man had been lying, with many others, around the pool, hoping that it would be stirred by the angel, and that he might be put into the water first, and so might be healed. There he waited long, and waited in vain. Why did he wait? Because Jesus was not there. Where Jesus is not, you must wait. If it is only an angel and a pool, you must wait; and one may get a blessing, and many may get no blessing. But when Jesus came, there was no waiting. He walked in among the crowd of sick folk, spied out this man, bade him take up his mattress and walk home, and he was healed at once.

Now, I commend this man for waiting. I admire him for his patience and his perseverance; but I beg you not to make his case your own. He waited, for Jesus was not there. You may not wait, you must not wait; for Jesus is here. There was necessity for him to wait. As I have told you, there was an angel and a pool, and nothing more; but where Christ is, there should be no waiting. Any soul that believes in Christ tonight will be saved tonight. Any soul that looks to Christ tonight shall be saved, even though he or she looks from the ends of the earth. You may look now; no, you are commanded to do so. "Behold, now is the accepted time; behold, now is the day of salvation." "Harden not your

---

This sermon was taken from *The Metropolitan Tabernacle Pulpit* and was preached on Sunday evening, February 16, 1890.

hearts, as in the provocation." There, in that pew, or in yonder aisles, if you turn your eye by faith to Jesus, the Living One on the throne of the Highest, you shall obtain immediate cure. Waiting is all very well at the pool of Bethesda; but waiting at the pool of ordinances, as I have heard some say, is not according to the Scriptures. I read nothing about waiting there; but I do read this, "Believe on the Lord Jesus Christ, and thou shalt be saved."

However, for the help of some who have waited until they are weary, who have persevered in the use of the means until they are becoming desponding and disappointed, let us look at this case of the impotent man at Bethesda.

The Savior Knew the Case

I only mention that in order to say that the Savior knows your case. *Jesus saw him lie there.* There were a great many objects for the Savior's eye to rest upon, but He fixed His gaze upon this man, long bedridden, thirty-eight years impotent. Even so, Jesus knows all about your case. He sees you lie just where you are tonight, impotent, without hope, without light, without faith. He sees you; I want you to feel this to be true. He singles you out amidst this throng, wherever you sit, and His eye is scanning you from head to foot; no, He looks within as well as without, and reads all that is in your heart.

Concerning the man at the pool, *Jesus knew that he had been a long time in that case.* He knows the years that you have been waiting. You remember being carried to the house of God by your mother. You recollect, as a child, listening to sermons that seemed to startle you; you went home to your little bedroom, and cried to God for mercy, but you forgot your impressions. They were like the morning mist that vanishes in the rising sun. You came to London; you grew to adulthood; you became careless about divine things; you shook off all your early impressions. Still, you went to hear the Word preached, and often you half hoped that you might get a blessing. You heard the Word, but faith was not mixed with what you heard, so you missed the blessing. Yet still you always had a wish that it should come to you. You never could despise godly people, or the things of Christ. You could not get them for yourself; at least, you thought you could not; but you always had some lingering wish that you were numbered with the people of God. Now, the Lord Jesus knows all about that, and the many years in which you have been waiting as a hearer, but a hearer only, and not a doer of the Word; impressed at times, but doing violence to your better feelings, and going back to a careless life. My Lord knows all about you. I cannot pick you out in this congregation, but remember, while I am preaching tonight, miracles will be wrought; processes which will change the very natures of people are going on within this house; Christ is being preached and His Gospel is being set forth and this is not done, with prayerful earnestness, in vain. God will bless it; He is going to bless somebody tonight. Who that somebody may be, or how many hundred somebodies there will be, I cannot guess; but He will bless His own Word, and why should He not bless you? He sees just who you are, and where you are, and what you are.

In addition to this, *our Lord knew all this poor man's disappointments.* Many times, when he had striven to get first to the water's edge, and did think that he should be able to take the happy plunge, in went someone else before him, and his hopes were gone. Another came up out of the water healed. Then, with a heavy sigh, he fell back upon his couch, and felt that it might be a long time before the angel stirred the water again, and even then he might be disappointed again. He recollected the many times when he had lost all hope, and there he lay almost in despair. Now I think I hear someone here tonight saying, "My brother found the Lord. My friend, who came with me here, found the Lord. I have lived to see my mother die in sure and certain hope of glory. I have friends who have come to Christ, but I am still living without Him. When there were special services, I hoped that I might have been specially blessed. I have been to prayer meetings, I have read my Bible in secret, and I have sometimes hoped—it was but a little hope, but still I hoped—'Maybe one of these days I may be healed.'" Yes, dear friend, and my Lord knows all about that, and He sympathizes in all the grief you feel tonight, and He hears those unspoken wishes of yours, and He knows your longing that you may be healed.

The Savior Aroused the Man's Desires

He said to him, "Wilt thou be made whole?" There he lay. I am not going to explain that lying at the pool, but just to apply it to you who are here in a similar condition.

Beware of forgetting why you are here. Beware of coming to the house of God and not knowing why you come. I have said that, years ago, you went to places of worship in the hope of finding salvation. Well, you have kept on coming, and you have not found it; but do you now look for it? Have you not fallen into the habit of sitting and listening to sermons, and prayers, and so on, without feeling that you came for anything special for yourself? You come and you go, merely that you may attend a place of worship; that is all. The Savior would not let the impotent man lie there satisfied because he was by the pool. No, no. He said to him, "Why are you here? Have you not some desire? Do you not want to be made whole?" My dear hearer, I wish that you were able to say yes to this question. Have you come here tonight that your sin

Impotence and Omnipotence 77

may be forgiven, that your soul may be renewed by divine grace, that you may meet with Christ? If so, I want to keep you to that point, and not to let you come and take a sitting here and come, and come, and come, and come and be just like the door on its hinges out there, which turns in and turns out again, and is not a bit the better for it. Oh, do not get into mere religious habits! Ritualistic habits they will be to you, simple as the ritual will be. You come, and you go, and you are satisfied. This will never do. Christ arouses your desire as He says, "Wilt thou be made whole?"

Also, *avoid a despairing indifference*. I remember two brothers and a sister who heard me preach for a considerable time, and they were in great distress of soul. But, at the same time, they had a notion that they could not believe in Christ, and that they must wait, I hardly know what for; and they did wait until they grew quite old. I did not know better people morally, or better hearers so far as interest in what they heard was concerned; but they never seemed to get any farther. At last they got into this state: they seemed to feel as though, if it was to be, it would be; and if it was not to be, it would not be; and that all that they could do was just to sit still, and be quiet and patient. Patient under the apprehension of being lost forever? Why, I do not expect the man in the condemned cell to be happy and patient when he hears them putting up his gallows! He must be concerned; he must be uneasy. I did my best to make these friends uneasy; but I confess that I fear my efforts were attended with very small results. The Savior said to this man, "Will you be made whole? You seem to be in such a state of indifference that you do not care whether you are made whole or not." No worse condition than that can be found; it is so hard to deal with. God save you from a sullen indifference in which you leave yourselves to drift to destruction at the will of some unknown fate!

I pray you to *remember that it is yours to will*, for Christ said to this man, "Will you be made whole? You cannot make yourself whole, but you can will and wish to be made whole." God's Holy Spirit has given to many of you to will and to do according to His good pleasure. You will never be saved against your will; God drags nobody to heaven by the ears. There must be in you a willing mind consenting to the work of His sovereign grace; if it be there, I want you to exercise it tonight, as Christ wished this man to exercise it: "Will you be made whole? Have you any wish that way, any desire or longing for healing?" I want to stir this fire, and make it burn; if there be only a spark of desire, I would breathe upon it, and pray the Holy Spirit to breathe upon it to make it into a great flame. Paul said, "To will is present with me; but how to perform that which is good, I find not." I believe that there are some here who have the will to be saved; God be thanked for that!

"Wilt thou be made whole?" I think that the Savior put this question for another reason, which I will turn into an exhortation. *Forego all prescribing as to how you are to be saved.* The question is not, "Will you be put into that pool?" but, "Will you be made whole?" The question is not, "Will you take this medicine? Will you that I should do this or that to you?" but, "Will you be made whole?" Have you come to this, that you are willing to be saved in God's way, in Christ's way? One says, "I want to have a dream." Dear soul, do not want any dreams; they are only dreams. Another says, "I want to see a vision." My dear friend, there is nothing in the plan of salvation about seeing visions. "I want to hear a voice," says one. Well, hear my voice, then, and may God the Holy Spirit make you to hear the voice of His Word through me! "But I want"—oh! yes, you want, you know not what you want, like many a silly child that has its fads, and fancies, and whims, and wishes. Oh, that all were willing to be saved by the simple plan of believe and live! If this is God's way, who are you that He should make a new way for you? When I had put the way of salvation before a friend, some time ago, she turned to me, and said, "Oh, sir, do pray for me!" "No," I said, "I will not pray for you." "Oh! but," said she, "how can you say that?" I replied, "I set before you Christ crucified, and I beg you to believe in Him. If you will not believe in Him, you will be lost; and I shall not pray God to make any different way of salvation for you. You deserve to be lost if you will not believe in Christ." I put it just so to her, and when she afterward said, "Oh, I see it now! I do look to Christ, and trust Him," I said, "Now I will pray for you; now we can pray together, and sing together, if need be." But, dear friends, do not set up your own notion about how you ought to be converted. Can you find any two people who were converted in the same way? God does not make converts as workers make steel pens, a gross in a box, all alike. No, no; but in each case there is a living person created, and every living person, every living animal, every living plant, is somewhat different from every other of its kind; you must not look for uniformity in the work of regeneration. "Wilt thou be made whole?" Come, do you desire the pardon of sin? Do you long for a new heart and a right spirit? If so, leave off disputing as to how you are to get them, and do what Christ tells you to do.

"Wilt thou be made whole?" It is as if the Savior said, *"Be more than ever in earnest now.* I know that you will to be made whole; will it more tonight than you have ever willed it before." Let the will which you have be exercised; put it forth. You are in earnest to be saved; be more in earnest tonight. You do desire to find Christ; well, desire to find Christ more tonight than ever you did in your life. You have come to an important crisis of your life; you may be at the point of death; who knows? How many have been suddenly struck down of late! If you would be made whole, I would that you might be made whole tonight. I pray that you may feel something pressing you, something that makes you end your long delay, something that makes you feel, "I have no more time to waste. I cannot afford to loiter. I must be saved tonight. I must hear the distinct ticking of God's great clock that stands in the hall of grace, and always says, 'Now; now; now; now; now'; and never utters any other sound." Oh, may the Lord make it to be so by His own free grace!

Thus, you see, the Savior aroused the desires of the man at the pool. First, He knew his case; and next, He aroused his desires.

The Savior Heard the Man's Plaint

This is what he said, "Sir, I have no man, when the water is troubled, to put me into the pool: but while I am coming, another steppeth down before me." Some of these people had kind friends who took turns at watching day and night, and the moment that the water was stirred, they took up their patient, and plunged him in. This man had lost all his friends; thirty-eight years of illness had worn them all out. He said, "I have no man to put me into the pool; how can I get into the water?" So there are many in this case; they want help. While I have been at Menton, I have had the joy of leading a number of friends to Christ. When I had to leave them and come back to London, one and another of them said to me, "What can we do without you, sir? We shall have nobody to lead us in the right way now; no one to instruct us, no one to meet our objections, nobody to solve our doubts, nobody to whom we can tell the anxieties of our hearts."

No doubt some of you would talk in the same fashion, and I must admit that *the lack of a helper is serious*. It is a great deprivation to have no one to help you in these things. Sometimes, if a friend will come up after the sermon and just say a kindly word, it will do more good than the sermon itself. Many a poor troubled one, who has been a long time in prison, might have been sooner released if only some kind friend had reminded the person of a divine promise which, like a key, would have opened the prison door. I agree with you that there is a great help in having an earnest Christian friend to lift you over a difficulty, to bear you down to the water's edge to which you cannot go by yourself and to put you into the pool. It is a great loss, certainly, if you have no such friend, and I am very sorry for you. You live in a village where there is nobody to speak to you about spiritual matters, or you attend a ministry that does not feed you. You have nobody to comfort you. There are not many, after all, who can really help sinners in coming to Christ. Some who try to do so are a great deal too wise, and others are too hardhearted. It wants special training in the school of grace if anyone is to learn to sympathize with others so as to be able really to help them. I can suppose that one here is saying, "I have no mother to speak to; I have no Christian friend in the family; I have no one to whom I can go for help; that is why I stick fast where I am."

Well, a helper is very valuable, but I want to say that *a helper may not be so valuable as you think*. I have known some who have had plenty of Christian helpers while they were seeking the Lord, but none of them were able really to help them. If you trust in earthly helpers and think them essential, God will not bless their efforts, and they will be of no use to you. I am afraid that many a seeker has had to say, even to good and earnest Christians, what Job said to his friends, "Miserable comforters are ye all." After all, how can a human being help you much in your soul's affairs? No person can give you faith or give you pardon; no person can give you spiritual life or even spiritual light. Though you have no one to help you, remember that you can make too much of people, and you can trust too much in Christian helpers. I beg you to recollect that. I am afraid that there are some professors who have been helped a little too much. They heard a sermon and were really impressed by it, and somebody was foolish enough to say to them, "That is conversion." It never was conversion at all. The friend further said, "Now, come forward, and make a profession." So they came forward, and made a profession of what they never had. Then the friend said, "Now, come to such a meeting; come and join the church. Come on." Thus they were led, and led, and led, never having any real internal life, or spiritual energy given them from on high. They are just like children in strollers, who are unable to walk alone. God save you from a religion that depends upon other people! There are some who have a kind of lean-to religion, resting on somebody else; when the support is taken away, what becomes of the lean-to? The good old lady who helped you for so many years dies; where is your religion then? The minister used to keep you going; you were like a whipping-top, and he like the whip that kept you spinning; when he is gone, where are you? Do not have a religion of that kind, I entreat you. Though a helper is very useful, remember that, under certain conditions, even a Christian helper may be a hinderer.

Now, my dear hearer, this is the point I have come to; you have to deal with Jesus tonight, and *dealing with Jesus, you need "no man."* You have not to deal with pools and angels; you have to deal with the Lord Jesus Himself. Suppose that there is no one to help you, do you want anyone when Jesus is here? The helper was wanted to put you into the pool; he is not wanted to introduce you to Christ. You may speak to Him yourself; you may sue for mercy for yourself; you may confess your sin yourself. You want no priest; you want a Mediator between your soul

Impotence and Omnipotence

and God, but you do not want any mediator between your soul and Jesus. You may come to Him where you are and as you are. Come to Him now; tell Him your case; plead with Him for mercy. He does not want my help; He does not want the help of the Archbishop of Canterbury; He does not want the help of anybody. He alone can meet your case. Just put your case into His hand; and then, if you have no one to be your helper, you need not lie down and fret about it, for He is able to save them to the uttermost that come to God by Him.

Now this is all very plain talk, but we want plain talk nowadays. I feel as if I had not preached on Sunday, unless I had tried to bring men and women to Christ. There are many high and sublime doctrines that I would like to speak of, and many deep and rapturous experiences that I would like to describe. Yet I feel that I must often leave these things, and keep to the much more commonplace, but much more useful matter of persuading people, in Christ's stead, that they look away from other people, and away from ordinances, and away from self, and deal with Jesus Himself distinctly and directly. For then there will be no need of human help, and certainly there will be no need of delay.

The Savior Met the Man's Case Entirely

This impotent man has no one to help him; Christ can help him without anyone. This man cannot move except with great pain. He has to crawl to the water's edge; but he need not crawl there, he need not move an inch. *The power to heal that man was in the Christ who stood there*, commissioned of God to save sinners and to help the helpless. Please to recollect that the power that saves, and all of it, is not in the saved individual, but in the Christ who saves. I take leave to contradict those who say that salvation is an evolution. All that ever can be evolved out of the sinful human heart is sin, and nothing else. Salvation is the free gift of God, by Jesus Christ, and the work of it is supernatural. It is done by the Lord Himself, and He has power to do it, however weak, no, however dead in sin, the sinner may be. As a living child of God, I can say tonight that—

> On a life I did not live,
> On a death I did not die,
> I stake my whole eternity.

You who would be saved must do the same; you must look right out of self to Him whom God has exalted to be a Prince and a Savior to humanity. The Christ met that man's case, for He was able to do anything for him that he required. He meets your case, my dear hearer, for He can do anything for you that is wanted. Between here and heaven's gate there shall never be anything required which He cannot give, or any help needed which He is not prepared to render, for He has all power in heaven and in earth.

Next, *the Lord can do more for you than you ask of Him.* This poor man never asked anything of Christ, except by his looks, and by his lying there at the pool. If you feel tonight as if you could not pray, if you have needs that you cannot describe, if there is something wanted, and you do not know what it is, Christ can give it to you. You shall know what it is that you want when you get it, but perhaps now, in His mercy, He does not let you know all your needs. But here is the point, He "is able to do exceeding abundantly above all that we ask or think." May He do it in you tonight! Take comfort from the cure of the impotent man, cherish hope, and say, "Why should He not also heal me?"

Now the way in which Christ worked was very singular. *He worked by a command.* It is not a way that you and I would have selected, nor a way of which some nominal Christians approve. He said to this man, "Rise." He could not rise. "Take up thy bed." He could not take up his bed; he had been thirty-eight years unable to get off his bed. "Take up thy bed, and walk." Walk? He could not walk. I have heard some objectors say, "That preacher says to people, 'Believe.' They cannot believe. He bids them 'Repent.' They cannot repent." Ah! well, our Lord is our example, and He said to this man who could not rise and could not take up his bed and could not walk, "Rise, take up thy bed, and walk." That was His way of exercising His divine power and that is the way in which Christ saves people today. He gives us faith enough to say, "Ye dry bones, hear the Word of the Lord!" They cannot hear. "Thus saith the Lord, Ye dry bones, live!" They cannot live, but they do hear, and they do live; while we are acting by faith, delivering a command which looks, upon the surface of it, to be absurd and unreasonable, the work of Christ is done by that command. Did He not say of old in the darkness, "Let there be light"? To what spoke the Lord that word of power? To darkness, and to nothingness. "And there was light." Now, He speaks to the sinner, and He says, "Believe, and live." He believes, and he lives. God wants those of His messengers who have the faith to give His command to let the sinner know that he has not the strength to obey, that he is morally lost and ruined, and yet to say, in the name of the eternal God, "Thus says the Lord, Rise, take up your bed, and walk. Believe, repent, be converted, and be baptized, every one of you, in the name of the Lord Jesus Christ." This is the way in which Christ's power goes forth to human beings. He said to the man with the withered hand, "Stretch forth thine hand," and he did so; He says to the dead, "Come forth," and they do come forth. His commandings are attended with enablings, and where His commands are faithfully preached, His power goes with them, and men and women are saved.

Impotence and Omnipotence

I close with this observation. *In obedience, power was given.* The man did not stop and wrangle with Christ, and say, "Rise? What do You mean? You look like a friend, but do You come here to make sport of me? Rise? Thirty-eight years have I been lying here, and You say, 'Rise.' Do You think that there has ever been a minute in those thirty-eight years in which I would not have gladly risen if I could have done so, and yet You say, 'Rise,' and You say, 'Take up your bed. Shoulder the rug on which you lie.' How can I do so? It is thirty-eight years since I could lift a pound weight, and You bid me shoulder this mat on which I lie. Do You make me a theme of jest? And walk? You say, 'walk.' Walk? Hear me, you sick ones around me, He tells me to walk! I can scarcely lift even a finger, yet He bids me walk!" Thus he might have argued the matter out, and it would have been a very logical piece of argument, and the Savior would have stood convicted of having spoken empty words.

Instead of speaking thus, no sooner did Christ say to him, "Rise," than he willed to rise; as he willed to rise, he moved to rise, and rise he did, to his own astonishment. He rose, and stooping down, rolled up his mattress, all the while filled with wonder, every part of his body singing as he rolled it up, and put it on his shoulder with alacrity. To his surprise, he found that the joints of his feet and legs could move, and he walked right away with his mattress on his shoulder, and the miracle was complete. Stop, man, stop! Come here! Now, had you the strength to do this of yourself? "No, not I. I lay there thirty-eight years; I had no strength until that word 'Rise,' came to me." But did you do it? "Oh! yes, you see that I did it. I rose, I folded up the mattress, and I walked away." But you were under some kind of compulsion that made you move your legs and your hands, were you not? "Oh! no; I did it freely, cheerfully, gladly. Compel me to do it? My dear sir, I clap my hands for joy to think that I could do it. I do not want to go back to that old mat and lie there again; not I." Then what did you do? "Well, I scarcely know what I did. I believed Him, and I did what He told me; and a strange, mysterious power came over me; that is the whole story." Now explain it; tell these people all about it. "Oh! no," says the man, "I know that it is so; but I cannot explain it. One thing I know, whereas I was a cripple, now I can walk; whereas I was impotent, now I can carry my bed; whereas I was lying there, now I can stand upright."

I cannot explain salvation to you tonight, or how it takes place; but I remember when I sat in the pew as despairing a sinner as ever lived. I heard the preacher say, "Look unto Christ, and live." He seemed to say to me, "Look! Look! Look! Look!" and I did look, and I lived. That moment, the burden of my sin was gone. I was crippled with unbelief no longer. I went home a sinner saved by grace to live to praise the Lord—

> E'er since by faith I saw the stream
> Thy flowing wounds supply,
> Redeeming love has been my theme,
> And shall be till I die.
>
> —*William Cowper*

I am impressed that I am going to have ever so many tonight who will just obey the Gospel command, "Believe, and live. Believe in the Lord Jesus Christ, and thou shalt be saved." Oh, do it. Do it now, and to God be glory, and to yourself be peace and happiness forever! Amen and Amen.

7
Carried by Four

And he withdrew himself into the wilderness, and prayed. And it came to pass on a certain day, as he was teaching, that there were Pharisees and doctors of the law sitting by, which were come out of every town of Galilee, and Judea, and Jerusalem: and the power of the Lord was present to heal them. And, behold, men brought in a bed a man which was taken with a palsy: and they sought means to bring him in, and to lay him before him. And when they could not find by what way they might bring him in because of the multitude, they went upon the housetop, and let him down through the tiling with his couch into the midst before Jesus. And when he saw their faith, he said unto him, Man, thy sins are forgiven thee. And the scribes and the Pharisees began to reason, saying, Who is this which speaketh blasphemies? Who can forgive sins, but God alone? But when Jesus perceived their thoughts, he answering said unto them, What reason ye in your hearts? Whether is easier, to say, Thy sins be forgiven thee; or to say, Rise up and walk? But that ye may know that the Son of man hath power upon earth to forgive sins, (he said unto the sick of the palsy,) I say unto thee, Arise, and take up thy couch, and go into thine house. And immediately he rose up before them, and took up that whereon he lay, and departed to his own house, glorifying God. And they were all amazed, and they glorified God, and were filled with fear, saying, We have seen strange things to day (Luke 5:16–26).

You have this same narrative in the ninth chapter of Matthew, and in the second chapter of Mark. What is three times recorded by inspired pens must be regarded as trebly important and well worthy of our earnest consideration. Observe the instructive fact that our Savior retired and spent a special time in prayer when He

---

This sermon was taken from *The Metropolitan Tabernacle Pulpit* and was preached on Sunday morning, March 19, 1871.

saw unusual crowds assembling. He withdrew into the wilderness to hold communion with His Father, and, as a consequence, to come forth clothed with an abundance of healing and saving power. Not but that in Himself as God He always had that power without measure; but for our sakes He did it, that we might learn that the power of God will only rest upon us in proportion as we draw near to God. Neglect of private prayer is the locust which devours the strength of the church.

When our Lord left His retirement He found the crowd around Him exceeding great, and it was as motley as it was great. For while here were many sincere believers, there were still more skeptical observers; some were anxious to receive His healing power, others equally desirous to find occasion against Him. So in all congregations, however the preacher may be clothed with his Master's spirit and his Master's might, there will be a mixed gathering; there will come together your Pharisees and doctors of the law, your sharp critics ready to pick holes, your cold-blooded cavilers searching for faults. At the same time, chosen of God and drawn by His grace, there will be present some devout believers who rejoice in the power that is revealed among humans, and earnest seekers who wish to feel in themselves the healing energy. It seems to have been a rule with our Savior to supply each hearer with food after his kind. The Pharisees soon found the matters to cavil at for which they were looking; the Savior so worded His expressions that they caught at them eagerly, and charged Him with blasphemy. The enmity of their hearts was thus thrown out upon the surface that the Lord might have an opportunity of rebuking it; had they been but willing, the power of the Lord was present to heal even them. Meanwhile, those poor tremblers who were praying for healing were not disappointed. The Good Physician passed by not a single case, and at the same time His disciples who were looking for opportunities of praising Him anew were also fully gratified, for with glad eyes they saw the paralytic restored and heard sins forgiven.

The case which the narrative brings before us is that of a man stricken down with paralysis. This sad disease may have been of long continuance. There is a paralysis which gradually kills the body, binding it more and more surely in utter helplessness. The nerve power is almost destroyed; the power of motion is entirely suspended; and yet the faculties of the mind remain, though greatly weakened, and some of them almost extinguished. Some have thought that this man may have been stricken with what is called the universal paralysis, which very speedily brings on death, which may account for the extreme haste of the four bearers to bring him near the Savior. We do not know the details of his case, but certain is it that he was paralyzed and, as I look at the case and study the three records, I think I perceive with equal clearness that this paralysis was in some way or other, at least in the man's own judgment, connected with his sin. He was evidently penitent as well as paralytic. His mind was as much oppressed as his bodily frame. I do not know that he could be altogether called a believer, but it is most probable that being burdened with a sense of sin he had a feeble hope in divine mercy, which, like a spark in smoking flax, had hard work to exist, yet was truly there. The affliction for which his friends pitied him was in his body, but he himself felt a far severer trouble in his soul, and probably it was not so much with the view of being healed bodily as in the hope of spiritual blessing that he was willing to be subjected to any process by which he might come under the Savior's eye. I gather that from the fact that our Savior addressed him in these words, "Be of good cheer," intimating that he was desponding, that his spirit sunk within him, and, therefore, instead of saying to him at once, "Rise, take up thy bed," our tenderhearted Lord said, "Son, thy sins be forgiven thee." He gave him at the outset a blessing for which the patient's friends had not asked, but which the man, though speechless, was seeking for in the silence of his soul. He was a "son," though an afflicted one; he was ready to obey the Lord's bidding when power was given, though as yet he could neither lift hand nor foot. He was longing for the pardon of sin, yet could not stretch out his hand to lay hold upon the Savior.

I intend to use this narrative for practical purposes; may the Holy Spirit make it really useful.

Some People Will Need the Aid of Others

This man must be born of four, so the Evangelist, Mark, tells us. There must be a bearer at each corner of the couch whereon he lay. The great mass of persons who are brought into the kingdom of Christ are converted through the general prayers of the church by the means of her ministry. Probably three out of four of the members of any church will owe their conversion to the church's regular teaching in some form or other. Her school, her pulpit, her press have been the nets in which they were taken. Private personal prayer has, of course, in many instances been mingled with all this, but still the most of cases could not be so distinctly traced out as to be attributable mainly to individual prayers or exertions. This is the rule, I think, that the Lord will have the many brought to Himself by the sounding of the great trumpet of jubilee in the dispensation of the Gospel by His ministers. There are some, again, who are led to Jesus by individual efforts, just as Andrew found his own brother Simon, so one believer by private communication of the truth to another person becomes instrumental, by the power of God's Spirit, in his conversion. One convert will bring another, and that other a third. But this narrative seems to show that there are cases which will neither be brought by the general preaching of the Word, nor yet by the instrumentality of one; they require that there should be two, or three, or four in holy combination, who, with one consent, feeling one common agony of soul, shall resolve to band themselves together as a company for this one object, and never to cease from their holy confederation until this object is gained and their friend is saved. This man could not be brought to Christ by one, he must have four to lend their strength for his carrying, or he cannot reach the place of healing.

Let us apply the principle. Yonder is a householder as yet unsaved. His wife has prayed for him long; her prayers are yet unanswered. Good wife, God has blessed you with a son who with you rejoices in the fear of God. Have you not two Christian daughters also? O you four, take each a corner of this sick man's couch and bring your husband, bring your father, to the Savior. A husband and a wife are here, both happily brought to Christ; you are praying for your children; never cease from that supplication: pray on. Perhaps one of your beloved family is unusually stubborn. Extra help is needed. Well, to you the Sabbath school teacher will make a third. He will take one corner of the bed; and happy shall I be if I may join the blessed quaternion, and make the fourth. Perhaps, when home discipline, the school's teaching, and the minister's preaching shall go together, the Lord will look down in love and save your child. Dear brother, you are thinking of one whom you have long prayed for; you have spoken to him also, and used all proper means, but as yet without effect. Perhaps you speak too comfortingly to him. It may be you have not brought that precise truth to bear upon him which his conscience requires. Seek yet more help. It may possibly be that a second brother will speak instructively where you have only spoken consolingly; perhaps the instruction may be the means of grace. Yet may it possibly happen that even instruction will not suffice any more than consolation, and it may be needful for you to call in a third who perhaps will speak impressively with exhortation and with warning, which may possibly be the great requisite. You two, already in the field, may balance his exhortation, which might have been too pungent by itself, and might have raised prejudice in the person's mind if it had come alone. All three of you together may prove the fit instruments in the Lord's hand. Yet when you three have happily combined, it may be the poor paralyzed one is not yet affected savingly. A fourth may be needed, who, with deeper affection than all three of you, and perhaps with an experience more suited to the case than yours, may come in, and working with you, the result may be secured. The four fellow-helpers together may accomplish, by the power of the Spirit, what neither one, nor two, nor three were competent to have done.

It may sometimes happen that someone has heard Paul preach, but Paul's clear doctrine, though it has enlightened the person's intellect, has not yet convinced his conscience. He has heard Apollos, and the glow of the orator's eloquent appeals has warmed his heart, but not humbled his pride. He has later still listened to Cephas, whose rough cutting sentences have hewn him down, and convinced him of sin; but before he can find joy and peace in believing, he will require to hear the sweet affectionate words of John. Only when the fourth shall grasp the bed and give a hearty lift will the paralyzed person be laid in mercy's path. I anxiously desire to see in this church little bands of men and women bound to each other by zealous love to souls. I would have you say to one another, "This is a case in which we feel a common interest. We will pledge each other to pray for this person; we will unitedly seek his salvation." It may be that one of our seat-holders, after listening to my voice these ten or fifteen years, is not impressed; it may be that another has left the Sabbath school unsaved. Let brotherly quaternions look after these by God's help. Moved by one impulse, form a square about these persons, beset them behind and before, and let them not say, "No man careth for my soul." Meet together in prayer with the definite object before you, and then seek that object by the most likely ways. I do not know, my brethren, how much of blessing might come to us through this, but I feel certain that until we have tried it we cannot pronounce a verdict upon it. Nor can we be quite sure that we are free from all responsibility to people's souls until we have tested every possible and probable method for doing them good.

I am afraid that there are not many, even in a large church, who will become sick-bearers. Many will say the plan is admirable, but they will leave it to others to carry it out. Remember that the four persons who join in such a labor of love ought all of them to be filled with intense affection to the persons whose salvation they seek. They must be men and women who will not shrink because of difficulty; who will put forth their whole strength to shoulder the beloved burden; and who will persevere until they succeed. They need be strong, for the burden is heavy; they need be resolute, for the work will try their faith; they need be prayerful, for otherwise they labor in vain; they must be believing, or they will be utterly useless—Jesus saw their faith, and therefore accepted their service; but without faith it is impossible to please Him. Where shall we find quartets such as these? May the Lord find them, and may He send them to some of you poor dying sinners who lie paralyzed here today.

Some People Will Need the Effort of Others

The essential means by which a soul is saved is clear enough. The four bearers had no question with each other as to what was the way to effect this man's cure. They were unanimous in this—that they must bring him to Jesus. By some means or other, by hook or by crook, they must place him in the Savior's way. That was undoubted fact. The question was, how to do this? There is an old worldly proverb, that "where there's a will there's a way." That proverb, I believe, may be safely imported into spiritual things, almost without a caution or grain of salt. "Where there's a will there's a way"; and if people be called of God's grace to a deep anxiety for any particular soul, there is a way by which that soul may be brought to Jesus; but that way may not suggest itself until after much consideration. In some cases the way to impress the heart may be an out-of-the-way way, an extraordinary way—a way which ordinarily should not be used and would not ordinarily be successful.

I dare say the four bearers in the narrative thought early in the morning, "We will carry this poor paralytic to the Savior, passing into the house by the ordinary door"; but when they attempted to do so the multitudes so blocked up the road that they could not even reach the threshold. "Make way; make way for the sick! Stand aside there, and give room for a poor paralyzed man. For mercy's sake, give a little space, and let the sick man reach the healing prophet!" In vain their entreaties and commands. Here and there a few compassionate persons back out of the crowd, but the many neither can nor will move; besides, many of them are engaged upon a similar business and have equal reasons for pressing in. "See," cries one of the four, "I will make way"; and he pushes and elbows himself a little distance into the passage. "Come on you three!" he cries. "Follow up, and fight for it, inch by inch." But they cannot do it; it is impossible; the poor patient is ready to die for fear as the bed is tossed about by the throng like a cockleshell boat on the sea waves; the patient's alarm increases, the bearers are distressed, and they are quite glad to get outside again and consider. It is evidently quite impossible by ordinary means to get him in.

What then? "We cannot burrow under the ground. Can we not go over the heads of the people, and let the man down from above? Where is the staircase?" Frequently there is an external staircase to the top of an Eastern house. We cannot be sure that there was one in this case; but if not, the next door house may have had such a convenience, and so the resolute bearers reached the top and passed from one roof to another. Where we have no definite information much may be left to conjecture. But this much is clear: by some means they elevated their unhappy burden to the housetop and provided themselves with the necessary tackle with which to let him down. The Savior was probably preaching in one of the upper rooms, unless the house was a poor one without an upper story. Perhaps the room was open to the courtyard which was crowded. At any rate, the Lord Jesus was under cover of a roof and a substantial roof too. No one who carefully reads the original will fail to see that there was real roofing to be broken through. It has been suggested as a difficulty that the breaking up of a roof might involve danger to those below, and would probably make a great smother of dust; and to avoid this, there have been various suppositions—such as that the Savior was standing under an awning, and the men rolled up the canvas; or that our Lord stood under a verandah with a very light covering, which the men could readily uncover. Others have even invented a trapdoor for the occasion. But with all due deference to eminent travelers, the words of the evangelists cannot be so readily disposed of.

According to our text, the man was let down through "tiling," not canvas, or any light material; whatever sort of tiling it was, it was certainly made of burnt clay, for that enters into the essence of the word. Moreover, according to Mark, after they had uncovered the roof, which, I suppose, means the removal of the "tiling," they *broke it up*, which looks exceedingly like breaking through a ceiling. The Greek word used by Mark, which is interpreted "breaking up," is a very emphatic word, and signifies digging through, or scooping up, which evidently conveys the idea of considerable labor for the removal of material. We are told that the roofs of Oriental houses are often made of big stones; that may be true as a general rule, but not in this case, for the house was covered with tiles; and as to the dust and falling rubbish, that may or may not be a necessary conclusion; but as clear as noonday is it that a substantial housetop, which required untiling and digging through, had a hole made in it, and through the aperture the man in his bed was let down.

Perhaps there was dust, and possibly there was danger too, but the bearers were prepared to accomplish their purpose at all risks. They must get the sick man in somehow. There is no need, however, to suppose either, for no doubt the four men would be careful not to incommode the Savior or His hearers. The tiles or plaster might be removed to another part of the flat roof, and the boards likewise, as they were broken up; and as for the spars, they might be sufficiently wide to admit the narrow couch of the sick man without moving any of them from their places. Mr. Hartley, in his *Travels*, says: "When I lived at Ægina I used to look up not infrequently at the roof above my head, and contemplate how easily the whole transaction of the paralytic might take place. The roof was made in the following manner—A layer of reeds of a large species was placed upon the rafters; on these a quantity of heather was strewed; on the heather earth was deposited and beaten down into a solid mass. Now, what difficulty would there be in removing first the earth, next the heather, and then the reeds? Nor would the difficulty be increased, if the earth had a pavement of tiling laid upon it. No inconvenience could result to the persons in the house, from the removal of the tiles and earth; for the heather and reeds would stop anything that might otherwise fall down, and would be removed last of all."

To let a man down through the roof was a device most strange and striking, but it only gives point to the remark which we have now to make here. If we want to have souls saved, we must not be too squeamish and delicate about conventionalities, rules, and proprieties, for the kingdom of heaven suffers violence. We must make up our minds to this: "Smash or crash, everything shall go to pieces which stands between the soul and its God. It matters not what tiles are to be taken off, what plaster is to be digged up, or what boards are to be torn away, or what labor, or trouble, or expense we may be at; the soul is too precious for us to stand upon nice questions. If by any means we may save some, is our policy. Skin for skin, yes, all that we have is nothing comparable to a human soul." When four true hearts are set upon the spiritual good of a sinner, their holy hunger will break through stone walls or house roofs.

I have no doubt it was a difficult task to carry the paralyzed man upstairs; the breaking up of the roof, the removing the tiling with all one care, must have been a laborious task and have required much skill, but the work was done, and the end was gained. We must never stop at difficulties; however stern the task, it must always be more difficult to us to let a soul perish than to labor in the most self-denying form for its deliverance.

It was a very singular action which the bearers performed. Who would have thought of breaking up a roof? Nobody but those who loved much, and much desired to benefit the sick. O that God would make us attempt singular things to save souls. May a holy ingenuity be excited in the church; a sacred inventiveness set at work for winning human hearts. It appeared to his generation a singular thing when John Wesley stood on his father's tombstone and preached at Epworth. Glory be to God that he had the courage to preach in the open air. It seemed an extraordinary thing when certain ministers delivered sermons in the theaters; but it is matter of joy that sinners have been reached by such irregularities who might have escaped all other means. Let us but feel our hearts full of zeal for God and love for souls, and we shall soon be led to adopt means which others may criticize, but which Jesus Christ will accept.

After all, the method which the four friends followed was one most suitable to their abilities. They were, I suppose, four strong fellows to whom the load was no great weight, and the work of digging was comparatively easy. The method suited their capacity exactly. And what did they do when they had let the sick man down? Look at the scene and admire? I do not read that they said a single word, yet what they did was enough: abilities for lifting and carrying did the needful work. Some of you say, "Ah, we cannot be of any use; we wish we could preach." These men could not preach: they did not need to preach. They lowered the paralytic, and their work was done. They could not preach, but they could hold a rope. We want in the Christian church not only preachers, but soulwinners, who can bear souls on their hearts and feel the solemn burden; those who, it may be, cannot talk, but who can weep; people who cannot break other's hearts with their language, but who break their own hearts with their compassion. In the case before us there was no need to plead "Jesus, You son of David, look up, for a man is coming down who needs You." There was no need to urge that the patient had been so many years sick. We do not know that the man himself uttered a word. Helpless and paralyzed, he had not the vigor to become a suppliant. They placed his almost lifeless form before the Savior's eye and that was appeal enough; his sad condition was more eloquent than words. O hearts that love sinners, lay their lost estate before Jesus; bring their cases, as they are, before the Savior. If your tongues stammer, your hearts will prevail; if you cannot speak even to Christ Himself as you would desire because you have not the gift of prayer, yet if your strong desires spring from the spirit of prayer you cannot fail. God help us to make use of such means as are within our power, and not to sit down idly to regret the powers we do not possess. Perhaps it would be dangerous for us to possess the abilities we covet; it is always safe to consecrate those we have.

The Root of Spiritual Paralysis Is Sin

Jesus intended to heal the paralyzed man, but He did so by first of all saying, "Thy sins are forgiven thee." There are some in this house of prayer this morning who are spiritually paralyzed. They have eyes and they see the Gospel; they have ears and they have heard it, and heard it attentively too; but they are so paralyzed that they will tell you, and honestly tell you, that they cannot lay hold upon the promise of God. They cannot believe in Jesus to the saving of their souls. If you urge them to pray, they say: "We try to pray, but it is not acceptable prayer." If you bid them have confidence, they will tell you, though not in so many words perhaps, that they are given up to despair. Their mournful ditty is—

> I would, but cannot sing;
> I would, but cannot pray;
> For Satan meets me when I try,
> And frights my soul away.
>
> I would, but can't repeat,
> Though I endeavor oft;
> This stony heart can ne'er relent
> Till Jesus makes it soft.
>
> I would, but cannot love,
> Though woo'd by love divine;
> No arguments have power to move
> A soul so base as mine.
>
> O could I but believe!
> Then all would easy be;
> I would, but cannot—Lord, relieve:
> My help must come from thee.

The bottom of this paralysis is sin upon the conscience, working death in them. They are sensible of their guilt, but powerless to believe that the crimson fountain can remove it. They are alive only to sorrow, despondency, and agony. Sin paralyzes them with despair. I grant you that into this despair there enters largely the element of unbelief, which is sinful; but I hope there is also in it a measure of sincere repentance, which bears in it the hope of something better. Our poor, awakened paralytics sometimes hope that they may be forgiven, but they cannot believe it; they cannot rejoice; they cannot cast themselves on Jesus; they are utterly without strength. Now, the bottom of it, I say again, lies in unpardoned sin, and I earnestly entreat you who love the Savior to be earnest in seeking the pardon of these paralyzed persons. You tell me that I should be earnest; so I should; and so I desire to be. But, brethren, their cases appear to be beyond the minister's sphere of action; the Holy Spirit determines to use other agencies in their salvation. They have heard the public word; they now need private consolation and aid, and that from three or four. Lend us your help, you earnest Christians; form your parties of four; grasp the couches of these who wish to be saved, but who feel they cannot believe. The Lord, the Holy Spirit, make you the means of leading them into forgiveness and eternal salvation. They have been lying a long time waiting. Their sin, however, still keeps them where they are. Their guilt prevents their laying hold on Christ. There is the point, and it is for such cases that I earnestly invoke my brothers' and sisters' aid.

Jesus Takes Away Both the Sin and the Paralysis

It was the business of the four bearers to bring the man to Christ; but there their power ended. It is our part to bring the guilty sinner to the Savior: there our power ends. Thank God, when we end, Christ begins, and works right gloriously. Observe that He began by saying: "Thy sins be forgiven thee." He laid the ax at the root; He did not desire that the man's sins might be forgiven, or express a good wish in that direction, but He pronounced an absolution by virtue of that authority with which He was clothed as the Savior. The poor man's sins there and then ceased to be, and he was justified in the sight of God. Believe this, my hearer, that Christ did thus for the paralytic man? Then I charge you believe something more, that if on earth Christ had power to forgive sins before He had offered an atonement, much more has He power to do this now that He has poured out His blood and has said, "It is finished," and has gone into His glory, and is at the right hand of the Father. He is exalted on high to give repentance and remission of sin. Should He send His Spirit into your soul to reveal Himself in you, you would in an instant be entirely absolved. Does blasphemy blacken you? Does a long life of infidelity pollute you? Have you been licentious? Have you been abominably wicked? A word can absolve you—a word from those dear lips which said, "Father forgive them, for they know not what they do." I charge you ask for that absolving word. No earthly priest can give it to you, but the great High Priest, the Lord Jesus, can utter it at once. You twos and fours who are seeking the salvation of men and women, here is encouragement for you. Pray for them now, while the Gospel is being preached in their hearing; pray for them day and night, and bring the glad tidings constantly before them, for Jesus is still able "to save to the uttermost them that come unto God by him."

After our blessed Lord had taken away the root of the evil, you observe He then took away the paralysis itself. It was gone in a single moment. Every limb in the man's body was restored to a healthy state; he could stand, could walk, could lift his bed, both nerve and muscle were restored to vigor. One moment will suffice, if Jesus speaks, to make the despairing happy, and the unbelieving full of confidence. What *we* cannot do with our reasonings, persuadings, and entreaties, nor even with the letter of God's promise, Christ can do in a single instant by His Holy Spirit, and it has been our joy to see it done. This is the standing miracle of the church, performed by Christ today even as aforetime. Paralyzed souls who could neither do nor will, have been able to do valiantly, and to will with solemn resolution. The Lord has poured power into the faint, and to them that had no might He has increased strength. He can do it still. I say again to loving spirits who are seeking the good of others, let this encourage you. You may not have to wait long for the conversions you aim at. It may be before another Sabbath ends the person you pray for may be brought to Jesus; or if you have to wait a little, the waiting shall well repay you, and meanwhile remember He has never "spoken in secret in a dark place of the earth." He has not "said unto the seed of Jacob, 'Seek ye me' in vain" (see Isa. 45:19).

Wherever Our Lord Works the Double Miracle, It Will Be Apparent

He forgave the man's sin and took away his disease at the same time. How was this apparent? I have no doubt the pardon of the man's sin was best known to himself; but possibly those who saw that gleaming countenance which had been so sad before might have noticed that the word of absolution sunk into his soul as the rain into the thirsty earth. "Thy sins be forgiven thee," fell on him as a dew from heaven; he believed the sacred declaration, and his eyes sparkled. He might almost have felt indifferent whether he remained paralyzed or not, it was such joy to be forgiven, forgiven by the Lord Himself. That was enough, quite enough for him; but it was not enough for the Savior, and therefore He bade him take up his couch and walk, for He had given him strength to do so. The man's healing was proved by his obedience. Openly to all onlookers an active obedience became indisputable proof of the poor creature's restoration. Notice, our Lord bade him rise—he rose; he had no power to do so except that power which comes with divine commands. He rose, for Christ said, "Rise." Then he folded up that miserable palliasse—the Greek word used shows us that it was a very poor, mean, miserable affair—he rolled it up as the Savior bade him, he shouldered it, and went to his home.

His first impulse must have been to throw himself down at the Savior's feet, and say, "Blessed be Your name"; but the Master said, "Go to thy house" and I do not find that he stayed to make one grateful obeisance, but elbowing the crowd, jostling the throng with his load on his back, he proceeded to his house just as he was told, and that without deliberation or questioning. He did his Lord's bidding, and he did it accurately, in detail, at once, and most cheerfully. Oh! how cheerfully; none can tell but those in like case restored. So, the true sign of pardoned sin, and of paralysis removed from the heart, is obedience. If you are really saved you will do what Jesus bids you. Your request will be, "Lord, what will You have me to do?" and that once ascertained, you will be sure to do it. You tell me Christ has forgiven you, and yet you live in rebellion to His commands; how can I believe you? You say you are a saved man, and yet you willfully set up your own will against Christ's will. What evidence have I of what you say? Have I not, rather, clear evidence that you do not speak the truth? Open, careful, prompt, cheerful obedience to Christ becomes the test of the wonderful work which Jesus works in the soul.

All This Tends to Glorify God

Those four men had been the indirect means of bringing much honor to God and much glory to Jesus, and they, I doubt not, glorified God in their very hearts on the housetop. Happy men to have been of so much service to their bedridden friend! Who else united in glorifying God? Why, first the man who was restored. Did not every part of his body glorify God? I think I see him! He sets one foot down to God's glory; he plants the other to the same note. He walks to God's glory; he carries his bed to God's glory; he moves his whole body to the glory of God; he speaks, he shouts, he sings, he leaps to the glory of God. When a man is saved his whole manhood glorifies God; he becomes infused with a newborn life which glows in every part of him—spirit, soul, and body. As an heir of heaven, he brings glory to the Great Father who has adopted him into the family. He breathes and eats and drinks to God's praise. When a sinner is brought into the church of God we are all glad, but we are none of us so joyous and thankful as he; we would all praise God, but *he* must praise him the loudest, and he will.

But who next glorified God? The text does not say so, but we feel sure that his family did, for he went to his own house. We will suppose that he had a wife. That morning when the four friends came and put him on the bed, and carried him out, it may be she shook her head in loving anxiety, and I dare say she said, "I am half afraid to trust him with you. Poor, poor creature, I dread his encountering the throng. I am afraid it is madness to hope for success. I wish you Godspeed in it, but I tremble. Hold well the bed; be sure you do not let him fall. If you do let him down through the roof, hold fast the ropes, be careful that no accident occurs to my poor bedridden husband; he is bad enough as he is, do not cause him more misery." But when she saw him coming home, walking with the bed on his back, can you picture her delight? How she would begin to sing, and praise and bless the Lord Jehovah Rophi, who had healed her beloved one. If there were little children about playing before the house, how they would shout for glee, "Here's father; here's father walking again, and come home with the bed on his back. He is made whole again as he used to be when we were very little." What a glad house! They would gather around him, all of them, wife and children, and friends and neighbors, and they would begin to sing, "Bless the Lord, O my soul: and all that is within me, bless his holy name. Bless the Lord, O my soul, and forget not all his benefits: who forgiveth all thine iniquities: who healeth all thy diseases." How the man would sing those verses, rejoicing in the forgiveness first, and the healing next, and wondering how it was that David knew so much about it, and had put his case into such fit words.

Well, but it did not end there. A wife and family utter but a part of the glad chorus of praise, though a very melodious part. There are other adoring hearts who unite in glorifying the healing Lord. The disciples who were around the Savior, they glorified God, too. They rejoiced, and said one to another, "We have seen strange things today." The whole Christian church is full of sacred praise when a sinner is saved; even heaven itself is glad.

But there was glory brought to God, even by the common people who stood around. They had not yet entered into that sympathy with Christ which the disciples felt, but they were struck by the sight of this great wonder, and they, too, could not help saying that God had wrought great marvels. I pray that onlookers, strangers from the commonwealth of Israel, when they see the desponding comforted, and lost ones brought in, may be compelled to bear their witness to the power of divine grace, and be led themselves to be partakers in it. There is "Glory to God in the highest, and on earth peace, good will toward men," when a paralyzed soul is filled with gracious strength.

Now, shall I need to stand here, and entreat for the four to carry poor souls to Jesus? Shall I need to appeal to my friends who love their Lord, and say, band yourselves together to win souls? Your humanity to the paralytic soul claims it, but your desire to bring glory to God compels it. If you are indeed what you profess to be, to glorify God must be the fondest wish and the loftiest ambition of your souls. Unless you are traitors to my Lord as well as inhuman to your fellowmen, you will catch the practical thought which I have striven to bring before you, and you will seek out some fellow Christians, and say, "Come, let us pray together, for such an one." If you know a desperate case, you will make up a sacred quaternion to resolve upon its salvation. May the power of the Highest abide upon you, and who knows what glory the Lord may gain through you? Never forget this strange story of the bed which carried the man, and the man who carried his bed.

8
The Free Agency of Christ

And he cometh to Bethsaida; and they bring a blind man unto him, and besought him to touch him. And he took the blind man by the hand, and led him out of the town; and when he had spit on his eyes, and put his hands upon him, he asked him if he saw ought. And he looked up, and said, I see men as trees, walking. After that he put his hands again upon his eyes, and made him look up: and he was restored, and saw every man clearly (Mark 8:22–25).

There is a very wonderful variety in the miracles of our Lord Jesus Christ, and the variety is apparent even in the way in which men come to Him to partake of His blessing. With regard to the blind men to whom our Lord gave sight, we read of some that they were brought to Christ by their friends, as in the case of this man at Bethsaida, who was almost passive all the way through. His friends appear to have had more faith than he himself had; therefore, they brought him to Jesus. There were other cases in which the blind men cried to Christ, and, as far as they could, came to Him of themselves. Some of them even came to Him in the teeth of stern opposition; for, when the disciples upbraided one of them for crying out so loudly, he cried out the more a great deal, "Thou Son of David, have mercy on me." So that, you see, some were brought to Christ by their friends, and others came to Him in spite of much opposition. Then there is that notable case, which many of you must remember, of that remarkable blind man, who had been blind from his birth, to whom Jesus came uninvited. Jesus saw him, and anointed his eyes with the clay which He had made, and then bade him go and wash in the pool of Siloam. "He went his way therefore, and washed, and came seeing." Thus, from the very commencement of our Savior's earthly ministry, there were

---

This sermon was taken from *The Metropolitan Tabernacle Pulpit* and was preached on Sunday evening, September 21, 1879.

differences in the way in which one class of characters, the blind, came to Jesus Christ.

There Are Great Differences in the Way in Which People Come to Jesus Christ

The lesson for us to learn from this undoubted fact is just this: there are great differences in the way in which people come to Jesus Christ, and differences even in their first desires. Some will begin to seek the Savior like merchants seeking goodly pearls; when they have found Him, He will be the pearl of great price to them. Others will be like the farmer whose plowshare struck against a crock of gold. They will know Christ's value as soon as they stumble upon Him, as it were, and will be ready to sell all that they have, and buy the field that the treasure may be theirs. Some of you who are here may get a blessing instantaneously, though you have not come especially seeking it. Others of you may have come here for months and years, seeking the Savior, and you may find Him now. Some may begin to seek even while the sermon is progressing, but may not find Christ for a while; others will no sooner seek Jesus than they will at once find Him. Some will be brought by the example of the godly, some by the preaching of the minister, some by a kind word from a friend, many by parental exhortations, some by a holy book, some by no outward means at all, some simply by their own thoughts in solitude or at the dead of night—all led by the one gracious Spirit of God, but each one brought to Christ in a different way, and by different means from all the rest.

I think that the same divergence will be found not only at the beginning of the Christian life, but also all the way through that life in all who are the subjects of divine grace. All Christians are like each other in some respects, but no one Christian is exactly like another in all points. There is, often, a great family likeness in the children in one family. Sometimes, you might go where there are ten or twelve, and you might pick them all out, and say, "Yes, we are quite sure that they all belong to this family. There are certain distinctive features which evidently show that they belong to these parents." After you have noticed that resemblance, take the ten or twelve children, one by one, and look at them individually. Perhaps, at first sight, you might say that you did not know one from the other. But those who see them day by day will tell you that there are distinct differences of countenance and contour about each one, and idiosyncrasies of character which distinguish them from one another, so that there is not one of them who is exactly like the rest. Now, it would be a great pity if they should all begin to wish that they were exactly like someone in the family whom they set up as a model. It would be a right and proper ambition that

The Free Agency of Christ

every son should wish to be like a godly father, and that every daughter should seek to imitate a lovely and gracious mother. But that one girl should wish to be just like her sister, or a boy to be exactly like his brother, would be absurd. Yet have I often seen that absurdity in the church of God. One is depressed because his experience is not quite like his neighbor's, another because he sees that there are points in his experience that are unlike anybody else's. I have even known them go and try to remove their names from God's register, and unchristianize themselves, and, what is worse, sometimes unchristianize one another, because they are not all exactly run into the same mold, like so many pennies, precisely alike in form and shape, as manufactured articles are when they come quickly from under the die. No; we fall into grievous error when we entertain this kind of idea. God's ways are diverse; from the beginning to the end, God the Father, God the Holy Spirit, and our Lord Jesus Christ, act sovereignly, and do not choose to follow one particular mode of action in every case.

That lesson I wish to teach, first, *in reference to our prayers.* We must not attempt to dictate to God with regard to His answers to our prayers. Let us learn that lesson from the incident before us: "They bring a blind man unto him, and besought him"—"to open his eyes"? No; that would have been a very proper prayer, but they "besought him to touch him." But Christ did not do His work according to their request: "He took the blind man by the hand, and led him out of the town; and when he had spit on his eyes, and put his hands upon him, he asked him if he saw ought." Now, with regard to our prayers, we may bring our children and friends and neighbors to Christ, and we may ask that they may be saved; but we must not dictate to Christ the methods by which salvation is to come to them, for it is very usual with Him not to follow those means which we would prescribe to Him. That plan of touching the sick person was a very common one with Christ, and therefore the people began to expect that He must always heal by a touch. Naaman thought that the prophet Elisha would come out to him, "and stand, and call on the name of the Lord his God, and strike his hand over the place, and recover the leper." But he was mistaken, as were those folk at Bethsaida. It was a sort of understanding among them that Christ's touch was the usual method by which His cures were wrought, so they besought Him to touch their blind friend; but He would not give any support to that notion. If they thought that He wrought His miracles by putting His hands upon the sick, then He would not put His hands upon them; He would let them see that He was not bound to any particular method. If He had allowed them to cherish such an idea, probably their next step in error would have been that they would have said that it was an enchantment, a kind of performance, by certain passes and touches, as by a wizard or conjurer, through which Christ went in order to heal the sick.

Superstition can be very easily made to grow; you and I, mark you, may think ourselves perfectly free from superstition, yet, all the while, it may only have taken some other form from that in which it appears in other people. For instance, if the Lord is pleased to bless a certain preacher to the conversion of souls, you may settle it in your mind that, if you get your children to hear him, they will assuredly be saved. Yet it may not be the case, for the Lord has a thousand ways of saving souls, and He is not tied to any one individual as His agent or instrument. It may get to be a kind of superstitious notion that in some one person alone the powers of converting others may rest. Or it may be that you say to yourself, "I was converted by reading such-and-such a book; if I get my boy to read that book, it will convert him, too." Yet it may have no influence whatever upon him, for the grace of God is not tied to any book, nor to any way of working that you choose to prescribe. I should not wonder, my dear friends, if some of you have tried to tie the Lord down to your way of working. For instance, in your class in the Sunday school, it was the reading of a certain chapter in the Bible that brought one of your scholars to Christ; so, in order to bring the rest of them to the Savior, you get them to read that chapter. That may be all right, for the Lord can bless it to them if He pleases, but at the same time you must remember that He is a Sovereign, and that therefore He will probably use other means in other cases. You preached, dear friend, in the street, or in the chapel, and God blessed that sermon; so you have made up your mind that you will preach it a second time. I recommend you not to do so, for very likely it will misfire if you do. If you begin to confide in the sermon, God will not bless it. I think it is often well to do with a good sermon as David did with Goliath's sword. He said that there was none like it, yet he did not keep it by him for constant use, but he laid it up before the Lord; then it was ready for the special occasion when it was required. When God has blessed any sermon that I have preached, I do not make it a rule to preach it again, lest I might be led to put my trust in that sermon, or to have some confidence in the way in which I set forth the truth rather than in the truth itself, though I never hesitate to preach the same sermon again and again if I feel that the Spirit leads me to do so. We must not, in our prayers, tie the Lord down to any particular means, for He can use what means He pleases, and He will do so whatever we may say. We may ask Him to open the blind man's eyes, but it is not our place to beseech Him to touch the blind man in order to effect His cure.

Notice, also, that Christ did not answer the prayer of these people in the place where they presented it. They brought the blind man to Him, and they evidently expected the Lord Jesus Christ to open his eyes there, but Jesus did not do so. "He took the blind man by the hand, and led him out of the town," right away from the place where the people wanted to have the miracle performed. The Savior acted as though He could not do anything in the matter until He was out of the town, and He would not speak a word to him until He got him quite away by himself. Well, now, it is very easy in our prayers to fix upon a certain place as the one where God will give His blessing, and to think, "The friend I am praying for must be converted in the Tabernacle, or must be converted in the little meeting that I hold in my house, or must be brought to Jesus Christ in the church where I attend, or in the chapel where I worship." But our Lord may, perhaps, never convert that young person in any one of the places you have mentioned; He may meet with him behind the counter, or on board ship, or walking by the way, or on a sickbed. Do not be disappointed, therefore, when your place does not prove to be God's place. Take your friend to the house of God, for Christ's miracles on a Sabbath day and in the synagogue are frequent; but do not try to tie Him down to the synagogue, for He must be left at liberty to work His miracles in His own way.

Neither, dear friends, must we, for a moment, try to tie the Lord Jesus Christ down *to work in our particular manner.* I have no doubt that these people meant to prescribe to Christ that He should open that man's eyes directly. He had done so before, and He was able to make the sightless one see in a single moment; they, therefore, naturally expected that He would do it. But the Savior did not do so; He did not work an immediate cure, but a progressive cure. He opened the man's eyes a little and afterward opened them more fully. This was a very extraordinary miracle; there is no other case like it in Scripture. All the other cures that Christ wrought were immediate, but this one was progressive. So, my friend, the Lord may hear and answer your prayer, but it may not be by a conversion in the way you expected. You thought that, on a sudden, you would hear that your dear friend had been turned from darkness to light. You have not heard that, but you have heard that he begins to be more thoughtful than he used to be, and that he attends the means of grace more regularly than he formerly did. Perhaps the Lord intends in his case to work salvation by degrees. Do not go and run the risk of spoiling it by trying to run faster than God guides you. The daylight does not always come in a moment. I am told that in the Tropics there is but slender notice of the rising of the sun; he seems to be up and shining in full glory in a few seconds. But here in England you know how long a time of twilight and dawn we have before the sun has fully risen. No doubt there are conversions that are just like the tropical morning; in a moment the great deed of grace is done.

But there are many more conversions that are slow and gradual, yet they are nonetheless sure. The genial sun is up when he is up—even if he takes an hour in the operation of rising—quite as effectually as he is up when he seems to leap out of the sea into meridian splendor. So, if the Lord should see fit to bless your friend in a different manner from that which you had thought of, do not you quarrel with Him. Whatever He does is right, so let us never question any of His actions.

One other point in which we must not dictate to God is this. *He may hear our prayer and grant our request, yet we may not know that it is so.* I do not think that these people who brought the blind man to Christ ever saw him again after his eyes had been opened. Mark tells us that Christ "led him out of the town," that is, away from his friends. After He had healed him, "he sent him away to his house, saying, Neither go into the town, nor tell it to any in the town." I suppose they found it out afterward, but there and then, at any rate, they did not see the man's eyes opened. If he did as Christ commanded him, he went straightaway home and kept the matter quiet, so far at least as the general public, and perhaps these friends of his also, were concerned. Now, it is quite possible that God may hear your prayer for some dear friend in whom you are interested and yet you may never know of it until you get to heaven. The Lord has promised to hear prayer, but He has not promised that you shall know that He has heard your prayer. A godly mother may be in glory long before her supplications have been answered in the conversion of her son. A Sunday school teacher may go home to be with Christ before the boys and girls over whom he or she has agonized are brought to the Savior. Our farmers know that earthly harvests are sometimes late, and it is the same in spiritual husbandry. Grace ensures the crop, but even the grace of God does not guarantee that the crop shall come up tomorrow, nor just whenever we please. So, dear friend, keep on sowing the good seed of the kingdom, water it with your tears and your prayers, and then leave with God the question whether you shall see the harvest or not. He may, in your case, fulfill that gracious promise, "He that goeth forth and weepeth, bearing precious seed, shall doubtless come again with rejoicing, bringing his sheaves with him"; or He may choose to make you simply the sower and another the reaper. It is for you to believe that your petitions shall be granted, even if you do not live to see it.

There have been many instances in which people's prayers have prevailed, although they themselves have never lived to see that happy result. I think I have told you, before now, the story of a godly father whose unhappy lot it was to see his children grow up without the fear of God in their hearts, and this was a very heavy burden upon the good old man's spirit. Day and night he wept and prayed about it before God. At last the time came for him to die, and he had not then one son or daughter who had found the Savior. It had been the old man's prayer that his death might be the means of the conversion of his children if they were not brought to Christ in his lifetime; and so it was. Yet the scene at his death was very different from what he had hoped that it might be, for it was a very gloomy departure. His faith was grievously tried, he did not enjoy the light of God's countenance. He was put to bed, as God often puts some of His best children to bed, in the dark. He died humbly trusting in Jesus, but not triumphing, not even rejoicing. He was in great pain of body and deep depression of spirit; his last thought was, "This experience of mine will only confirm my children in their infidelity. I have born no witness for Christ as I had hoped to do; now they will say that their father's religion failed him at the last; my heart's desire will not be granted to me." Yet it was granted, though he did not live to see it; for after they had put him in the tomb and had come home from the funeral, the eldest son said to the others, "You noticed, brothers, what a struggle our father seemed to have on his dying bed and how hard it went with him. Now, we all know that he was a man of God; his conduct and example were such that we have no doubt about his being a true Christian. Yet, if he found it so hard to die, what will it be for each of us when we come to the day of our death and have no God to help us, and no Christ to look to in the hour of our extremity?" It was remarkable that the same thought had struck all the good man's children, and they went to their own homes, deeply impressed by their father's gloomy death, to seek their father's God and to find Him. Could the old man have known what was best, he would have chosen just such a death in order that he might, thereby, be the means of bringing his children to Christ.

In like manner, you may not be sure that you will see here the answer to all your prayers, but you will see it when you get up yonder. When God shall bid you fling up the celestial windows, and you will look down, and see the harvests which you never reaped, but for which you sowed the seed. You will see upspringing from the soil the rich result of your labor, though you saw it not while here on earth. Your heaven will be all the sweeter because, then, you will know that the Lord has heard and answered the prayers that you offered in your lifetime here below.

We Must Not Attempt to Tell the Lord Jesus Christ How He Is to Work

The Lord has various ways of working in the blessing of men and women. For instance, when this blind man was brought to Him, *He did not open his eyes with a word.* Often, when the sick were brought to Him, He spoke, and they were at once cured. He might have done so in this case; He might have said to the blind man's eyes, "Be opened!"

The ancient fiat might have been repeated, "Light be!" and there would have been light in his darkness. But there came out of Christ's mouth— not a word, but spittle! Christ spat on the blind man's eyes. Ah! but, if anything comes out of *His* mouth, it does not matter much what it is; whatever comes out of the mouth of the Christ of God means healing and life to those whom it reaches. He has His own ways of working. Usually, He is pleased to save people by the preaching of the Word, and sometimes the great change is brought about through very feeble testimony. Nevertheless, it is the Word of the Lord that is spoken, and it comes from the mouth of God, so He blesses it to the opening of blind eyes.

In this case, too, *Christ did not work upon this man all at once.* As I have already reminded you, He wrought a gradual cure upon him. So, dear friend, you must not yourself dictate to Jesus Christ as to how you will be saved. I know that some of you do. One said to me in my vestry that she believed she had found Christ, but she was half afraid it could not really be so. "Why not?" I asked. She answered, "My old grandfather told me that it took him three years before he got peace, and he was locked up in a lunatic asylum most of the time. I thought it was an awful affair altogether." I inquired where she could find anything in the Word of God to support that idea, and then told her simply to believe in the Lord Jesus Christ and not to trouble about what her grandfather did. I have no doubt that he got to heaven even through a lunatic asylum— but there are other and better ways of getting there.

Mr. Bunyan tells us that his pilgrim went through the Slough of Despond, and did not pick the steps well, so he floundered, and it was with difficulty that he got to the other side. Mr. Bunyan pictures Evangelist as bidding the poor seeker fly toward a certain wicket gate and keep his eye on the light within that gate. Now, that was a mistake on the part of Evangelist, and it was through that mistake that the poor pilgrim got into the Slough of Despond. The Gospel does not tell you to look out for wicket gates, nor to keep your eye on any light. You remember how, at last, the poor pilgrim did get rid of his burden; it was at the cross that the burden rolled from his shoulders and disappeared into the sepulcher so that he saw it no more. Dear friends, that is where your eye has to be turned—to the Cross of Christ, and to the full atonement He has made for all who trust in Him. As for wicket gates, and the Slough of Despond, the less you have to do with them, the better. "But is there no Slough of Despond?" someone asks. Oh, yes! twenty of them; but it is far easier to go through that Slough with the burden off rather than on your shoulders. The best thing you can possibly do is to go to Christ first, for then you can better go wherever you have to go. As for me, I would rather avoid the Slough of Despond altogether if I

The Free Agency of Christ

could and keep my eye ever upon the Cross, for Christ crucified is the one and only hope of sinners.

You must not any of you say, "Bunyan went through the Slough of Despond; according to his *Grace Abounding*, he was there for years. There is our pastor, I have often heard him say that he was a long while in that Slough." Yes, I am sorry to say that he was, but that is no reason why you should go there. If, when I was a youth, I had heard the Gospel of Christ preached as plainly as I have preached it to you, I feel certain that I would never have been in the bog so long as I was. But I heard a mixed sort of gospel, a mingle-mangle—a mixture of law and gospel—a muddling up of Moses and Christ—something of "do" and something of "believe"; therefore, I was for so long a time in that sad state of bondage. In fact, the good sound-doctrine people that I used to hear said, "You must not come to Christ, for you do not know whether you are one of the elect, and you must not come until you do." I how perfectly well that nobody can possibly tell whether he is elect or not until he finds it out by coming to God, and that no one ever comes to God the Father, who makes the election, except by Jesus Christ His Son. So we have first to do with the Son and afterward with the Father. That I did not know when I was seeking the Savior. I wanted an angel to tell me that I was one of the elect, but I was obliged to come to Christ as a poor, guilty sinner, and just trust in Him, and so to find peace in believing. That is the plan that I would recommend you to adopt if you want to be saved. Do not say, "I shall not come to Christ until I stick in the mud of the Slough of Despond; I shall not come to Him until I get laid by the heels in Giant Despair's Castle; I shall not come to Him until I get whipped on the back with the ten-thonged lash of the Law." If you really want to have that lash, perhaps you will get it, and I hope you will like it; but the Gospel says, "Come and welcome! Come and welcome! Come to Jesus just as you are!" Never try to lay down rules and regulations for Christ, but let Him save you in His own way; be content, just as you are, to take Him just as He is.

There is one more point about this man in which the singular sovereignty of Christ is seen, and that is, *He did not make use of the healed man*, though we would have thought that He would have done so. If this miracle had been wrought in the present day, we would soon have seen this man in the Salvation Army or in some other public position. Nowadays the rule seems to be, send off a paragraph to the newspapers, "So many in the inquiry room; so many converted on such-and-such a night." Blow the trumpets! Beat the drums! Let everybody know! But that was not Jesus Christ's way of working. He told this man not to go into the town, and when he did get home, not to tell anybody what had been done to him. Why was he not to tell anybody? Well, first, because the Lord wanted to do good and not to have a noise made about it. Secondly, because there was no need to tell anybody. Suppose I had been for years a blind preacher and that my eyes had been opened, would there be any need for me to tell you next Sunday that my eyes were opened? You would see it for yourselves; everybody can see when a person's eyes are opened. And, often, the best way in which a person can tell that he is converted is simply by letting other people see what a change there is in him, because if his eyes are not really open, it is of no use for him to stand up and say, "Bless the Lord! my eyes are open," while he is still blind. I have heard people say that they were converted, and I have thought that if the work were done over again, it would not hurt them much; and that, indeed, six or seven such conversions would not amount to much. Oh, give us a conversion that speaks for itself! Give us a new heart that shows itself in a new life. If a man is not able to control his temper or to speak the truth—if he is not a good servant, or a good master, or a good husband—do not let him think it necessary to proclaim what Christ has done for him; for if He has done anything that was worth doing, it will speak for itself.

Now I must close by just noticing one fact about this man as to the early steps that Jesus Christ used with him. There is one point I want to dwell upon for a minute. Our Lord, before He did anything else with the blind man, took him by the hand and led him out of the town. There are some of you here, perhaps, with whom the Lord has been thus working; you have begun to come to listen to the Gospel—through your wife, perhaps, or through some Christian friend. I am very hopeful concerning you, for, although you cannot yet see, the Lord has taken you by the hand. All the faith that this poor man had was a yielding faith; he gave himself up to be led, and that is a saving faith. My dear friend, give yourself up to be led by Christ now. If you have come under gracious, heavenly influences, yield yourself up to them.

The Master led this blind man right away from other people, and it will be a good sign when you begin to feel that you are getting to be lonely. Sometimes, when the Lord means to save someone, He lays him aside by illness; or, if not, He takes him away from the company he used to keep by some other means; or if the person is allowed to go into the same company, he gets to dislike it. He does not feel at home with those who were once his boon companions. He goes in and out of the shop as if he were one by himself. He has the Lord's arrow sticking in him, and like the wounded stag he tries to get away to bleed alone. You feel sometimes as though nobody understands you. You read in the Book of Job, or the Lamentations of Jeremiah, and you say, "This is the kind of experience that I am passing through. I have a broken heart, and a troubled conscience, and I feel that I am all alone." Well, dear friend,

The Free Agency of Christ

that is the Lord Jesus Christ leading you out of the town, getting you away from everybody. And, mark you, the place of mercy is the place where a person stands alone—away from everybody except his Lord. Do not draw your hand back from the hand that is leading you away. Perhaps ungodly company has been your ruin, and it is through solitude that God intends to save you. Be much alone; think over your own case. Make a personal confession of sin. Seek for personal faith in a personal Savior. You were born alone; you will have to pass through the gates of death alone. Although you will stand in a crowd to be judged, yet you will be judged as a separate individual, and even though myriads perish with you, your loss will be your own if you are lost. Therefore, look into your own affairs; cast up your own account; before the living God, stand separate from all your fellowmen. I believe that if any of you have reached that point you are where the deed of grace shall be done. May the Lord enable you to yield yourself up completely to Him, for your safety lies there! We rightly put faith before you as a look; but now I will put it before you, if you have not even an eye to look with, as the yielding up of yourself to the guidance of the Savior. Be nothing, and let Christ be everything. Give yourself entirely up into His hands, and He must and will save you, for that, though it be faith in its passive form, is, nevertheless, a real and saving faith, and blessed are all they that have it. May God grant it to everyone of us now, for Jesus sake! Amen.

9

The Two Draughts of Fishes

Now when he had left speaking, he said unto Simon, Launch out into the deep, and let down your nets for a draught (Luke 5:4).

And he said unto them, Cast the net on the right side of the ship, and ye shall find. They cast therefore, and now they were not able to draw it for the multitude of fishes (John 21:6).

The whole life of Christ was a sermon. He was a prophet mighty in word and deed; by His deeds as well as His words He taught the people. It is perfectly true that the miracles of Christ attest His mission. To those who saw them they must have been evident proof that He was sent of God. But we ought not to overlook that probably a higher reason for the miracles is to be found in the instruction which they convey. To the world without, at the present time, the miracles of Christ are harder to believe than the doctrine which He taught. Skeptics turn them into stones of stumbling, and when they cannot cavil at the marvelous teaching of Jesus, they attack the miracles as monstrous and incredible. I doubt not that even to minds seriously vexed with unbelief, the miracles, instead of being helps to belief, have been trials of faith. Few indeed are there in whom faith is wrought by signs and wonders, nor indeed is this the Gospel way of bringing conviction to the soul. The secret force of the living Word is the chosen instrumentality of Christ, and wonders are left to be the resort of that antichrist by whom the nations shall be deceived. We, who by grace have believed, view the miracles of Christ as noble attestations to His mission and divinity, but we confess that we value them even more as instructive homilies than as attesting witnesses. It is our conviction that we would lose much of the benefit which they were meant to convey to us if we were

---

This sermon was taken from *The Metropolitan Tabernacle Pulpit* and was preached on Sunday morning, April 6, 1862.

The Two Draughts of Fishes

merely to view them as seals to the roll, for they are a part of the writing of the roll itself. The marvels wrought by our blessed Lord are acted sermons fraught with holy doctrine, set forth to us more vividly than it could have been in words. We start with the assumption upon which our sermon will be grounded this morning, that Christ's miracles are sermons preached in deeds, visible allegories, truths embodied, principles incarnated and set in motion. They are the pictures in the great book of Christ's teaching, the illustrations by which He flashed light into dim eyes.

We have heard of some ministers who could say that they had often preached from the same text, but they had never delivered the same discourse. The like may be said of Christ. He often preached upon the same truth, but it was never precisely in the same manner. We have read in your hearing this morning the narrative of two miracles, in Luke 5 and John 21, which seem to the casual observer to be precisely alike. But he who shall read diligently and study carefully, will find that though the text is the same in both, yet the discourse is full of variations. In both the miraculous draughts of fishes, the context is the mission of the saints to preach the Gospel—the work of man catching—the ministry by which souls are caught in the net of the Gospel, and brought out of the element of sin to their eternal salvation.

The preacher is compared to a fisherman. The fisherman's vocation is a toilsome one; woe be to that minister who finds his calling to be otherwise. The fisherman must go forth in rough weathers and at all hazards; if he would only fish in a calm sea he may starve. So the Christian minister, whether people will receive the word with pleasure or reject it with anger and wrath, must be ready to imperil reputation and risk comfort. Yes, he must hate his own life also, or he is not worthy of the heavenly calling. The fisherman's is a rough occupation; no dainty fingers may come in contact with his nets. It is not a trade for gentlemen, but for rough, strong, fearless men, who can heave a rope, handle a tar brush, or scour a deck. The ministry is not meant for your dainty souls who would go delicately through this world without a trial, an offense, an insult, or a sneer. Such work is meant for men and women who know how to do business on great waters and can go abroad upon the sea not fearing the spray or the waves. The fisherman's calling, too, must be carried on perseveringly. It is not by one grand haul that a man makes his fortune, he must constantly cast forth his net. One sermon makes not a preacher; he who shall but now and then deliver himself of some carefully prepared oration is no true minister of God. He must be instant in season and out of season. He must cast his net in all waters; he must in the morning be at his work, and in the evening he must not withhold his hand. To be a fisherman a man must expect disappointments; he must often cast in the net and bring up nothing but weeds. The minister of Christ must reckon upon being disappointed; and he must not be weary in well doing for all his disappointments, but must in faith continue in prayer and labor, expecting that at the end he shall receive his reward. It needs no great labor for you to work out at leisure the comparison between fishermen and the Gospel ministry, the simile is so aptly chosen.

The two narratives before us have a degree of uniformity; this shall be our first point. *But they have a greater degree of dissimilarity;* we will bring that out in the second place. And, then, thirdly, we will suggest *some great lessons which they both combine to teach us.*

In These Two Miracles There Are Many Points of Uniformity

First you will perceive that in both miracles we are taught that *the means must be used.* In the first case, the fish did not leap into Simon's boat to be taken; nor, in the second case did they swarm from the sea and lay themselves down upon the blazing coals that they might be prepared for the fisherman's feast. No, the fishermen must go out in their boats, they must cast the net and after having cast the net, they must either drag it ashore or fill both boats with its contents. Everything is done here by human agency. It is a miracle, certainly, yet neither the fisherman, nor his boat, nor his fishing tackle are ignored; they are all used and all employed. Let us learn that in the saving of souls God works by means; that so long as the present economy of grace shall stand, God will be pleased by the foolishness of preaching to save them that believe. Every now and then there creeps up in the church a sort of striving against God's ordained instrumentality. I marked it with sorrow during the Irish Revival. We constantly saw in some excellent papers remarks which I thought exceedingly injurious, wherein it was made a subject of congratulation that no man was concerned in the work, no eminent preacher, no fervent evangelist; the whole was boasted to be conducted without human instrumentality. That was the weakness of the Revival, not its strength. You say it gave God the more glory. Not so. God gets the most glory through the use of instruments. When God works without instruments, doubtless He is glorified; but He knows Himself in which way He gets the most honor, and He has Himself selected the plan of instrumentality as being that by which He is most magnified in the earth. We have this treasure. How? Alone? Without any earthly accompaniment? No; but in earthen vessels. What for? That God may have less glory? No; but in the earthen vessels on purpose "that the excellency of the power may be of God," and not of us. God makes the infirmity of the creature to be the foil to the strength of the Creator. He takes people who are nothing in themselves and works by them His splendid victories.

Perhaps we would not admire Samson so much if he had dashed the Philistines in pieces with his fist, as we do since with the jawbone of an ass he laid on heaps the thousands of his foes. The Lord takes ill weapons that with them He may work great deeds. When He said, "Let there be light," and there was light without any instrument, He showed His glory; but when instead thereof He takes the apostles and says again, "Let there be light," and sends *them* forth who were darkness in themselves, and makes them the medium of lighting up a dark world, I say there is a greater glory. If the morning stars sang together when they first saw light upon the new-made earth, surely the angels in heaven rejoiced yet more when they saw light thus streaming upon the dark earth through men, who, in and of themselves, would only have increased the blackness and made the gloom more dense. God works by means of men and women whom He especially calls to His work, and not, as a rule, without them. The Plymouthist strives to get rid of the pastorate, but he never can, for the Lord will ever continue to give pastors after His own heart to feed His people, and all attempts made by the flock to dispense with these pastors will lead to leanness and poverty of soul. The outcry against the "one-man ministry" comes not of God, but of proud self-conceit, of people who are not content to learn although they have no power to teach. It is the tendency of human nature to exalt itself that has raised up these disturbers of the peace of God's Israel, for they will not endure to submit themselves to the authorities which God has Himself appointed, and they abhor the teachings of the apostle where he says by the Spirit of God, "Obey them that have rule over you, and submit yourselves: for they watch for your souls, as they that must give account, that they may do it with joy, and not with grief: for that is unprofitable to you." Friends, I warn you, there is a spirit abroad which would pull down those whom God Himself has raised up, that would silence those into whose mouths God has put the tongue of fire, that the foolish might prate according to their own will to the profit of no one, and to their own shame.

As for us, we shall, I trust, never cease to recognize that agency by which the Lord works mightily among us. We would check no ministry in the church of God. We would be but too glad to see it more abundantly exercised. Would God that all the Lord's servants were prophets! But we enter our solemn protest against that spirit which, under pretense of liberty to all, sets aside the instrumentality by which the Lord especially works. He will have you still keep the fishermen to their nets and to their boats; your new ways of catching fish without nets and saving souls without ministers will never answer, for they are not of God. They have been tried, and what has been the result of the trial? I know not a church that has despised instrumentality that has not come to an end within a few years, either by schism or decay. Where upon the face of the earth is there a single church that has existed fifty years where God's chosen instrumentality of ministry has been despised and rejected? "Ichabod!" is written upon their walls. God rejects them because they reject God's chosen way of working. Their attempts are flashes in the pan, meteoric lights, will-o'-the-wisps, swellings of proud flesh, bubbles of foam, here today and gone forever on the morrow.

Again, in both our texts there is another truth equally conspicuous, namely, that *means, of themselves, are utterly unavailing.* In the first case you hear the confession, "Master, we have toiled all the night and have taken nothing." In the last case you hear them answer to the question, "Children, have ye any meat?" "No"—a sorrowful No. What was the reason of this? Were they not fishermen plying their special calling? Verily, they were no raw hands; they understood the work. Had they gone about the toil unskillfully? No. Had they lacked industry? No, they had *toiled.* Had they lacked perseverance? No, they had toiled *all the night.* Was there a deficiency of fish in the sea? Certainly not, for as soon as the Master comes there they are by shoals. What, then, is the reason? Is it not because there is no power in the means themselves apart from the presence of Christ? The Great Worker who does not discard the means would still have His people know that He uses instrumentality, not to glorify the instrument, but for the sake of glorifying Himself. He takes weakness into His hands and makes it strong, not that weakness may be worshiped, but that the strength may be adored which even makes weakness subservient to His might. Brothers and sisters, let us as a church always keep this in mind, that without Christ we can do nothing. "Not by might, nor by power, but by my Spirit, saith the Lord." Put no dependence upon societies, upon committees, upon ministries, upon anything that we can do. Let us work as if it all depended upon us; but let us come to God depending upon Him, knowing of a surety that it does not rest with us, but with Him alone. Let us send forth the missionaries to the heathen; let us send forth our men into the dark streets and lanes of London; let us scatter tracts; let us distribute the Word of God; let us send forth preachers by scores from our "School of the Prophets." But when this is done, let us not sit still and say, "Now it is all accomplished, good must come of it." No, Lord, unless Your blessing descend from on high, as well might we have done nothing, for no eternal results can follow.

How often this drives me to my knees. The surprising work which God is doing in connection with this place lifts up my heart with joy; but then the fear lest it all should come to nothing for lack of His blessing casts my spirit to the very earth. You will remember, I dare say, that one brother was moved some time ago to distribute a volume of the

The Two Draughts of Fishes

sermons preached here to every student in Oxford and Cambridge. After that had been done and some two hundred thousand sermons had been distributed, he then gave them to every member of Parliament, to every peer of the realm, and to princes, kings, and emperors of Europe, and having accomplished that work, he has another in hand of great magnitude. Dear friends, as I think of these books traveling everywhere among high and low, the rich and poor in all places of the land, my heart is glad. But then, if God withholds the blessing, as well had they never been born in the press and circulated by human hand. What good can they do? Let the net be ever so broad, ever so strong, and let it be ever so industriously cast into the sea, yet we shall toil all the night and take nothing unless the Master comes to own the work. Let us, then, be always in prayer for the blessing. Let us remember that we have done nothing until we have prayed over what we have done; let us consider that all the seed we have put into the ground is put there for worms to eat unless we have dropped into the soil the preserving grain of prayer to keep that other grain alive. We shall have harvests if we wait on God for them. But after all our sowing, if we look to the soil, the seed, or the sower, we shall see nothing for our pains.

    Thirdly, there is clearly taught in both these miracles the fact that it is *Christ's presence that confers success*. Christ sat in Peter's boat. His will by a mysterious influence drew the fish to the net, as though He had a hook, a secret hook in each of their jaws, could stop them in their sportive leapings, and hurry them all to one common center. It was His presence on the dry land, when He spoke from off the shore to His toiling disciples out yonder, and said "Cast the net on the right side of the ship"—it was His presence that drew the fish to the place where they were taken. Oh, friends, we must learn this—that it is Christ's presence in the midst of the church that is the church's power—the shout of a King in the midst of the church that is the church's power—the shout of a King in the midst of her. It is the presence of Christ's great representative, the Holy Spirit, that is to give the church force. "I, if I be lifted up, will draw all men unto me." There is the attraction. The Spirit gives the power, and we must tarry until we get it; but when we have it, then we cannot preach in vain, for we become "a savor of life unto life" to those who hear. Christians, Christ's presence with you must be your power. Be much in fellowship with Him; catch much of His Spirit; meditate much upon His sufferings; keep close to His person; then, wherever you go there shall be a power about you which even your adversaries shall be compelled to acknowledge. Oh, that we had more of Christ's presence in us as a church! Lift up your hearts for it. If Christ be here at all, let us not grieve Him. "I charge you, O ye daughters of Jerusalem, that you stir not up nor awake my love until he please." And if He be not here let us rise form the bed of our sloth and go forth and seek Him, crying, "Oh thou whom my soul loveth, tell me where thou feedest, where thou makest thy flock to rest at noon!" And if you find Him, I charge you hold Him, and let Him not go until you bring Him into our mother's house, into the chamber of her that bare us, even the church of Christ. There will we hold Him, there will we embrace Him, and He shall show to us His loves.

In both instances *the success* which attended the instrumentality through Christ's presence *developed human weakness.* We do not see human weakness more in unsuccess than in success. In the first instance, in the success you see the weakness of the men, for the net breaks and the ships begin to sink, and Simon Peter falls down with— "Depart from me for I am a sinful man, O Lord." He did not know so much about that until his own boat was filled; but the very abundance of God's mercy made him feel his own nothingness. In the last case, they were scarcely able to draw the net because of the multitude of fishes. Friends, if you or I would know to the fullest extent what utter nothings we are, if the Lord shall give us success in winning souls we shall soon find it out. As we see first one, and then another, and then scores, and then hundreds brought to the Lord Jesus, we shall say, "Who hath begotten me these? How can such wonders be wrought by me?" And we shall fall prostrate before the footstool of sovereign grace, and confess that we are unworthy of such amazing favors. Let the church spread, let her conquests be many, let her overrun whole provinces with her heavenly arms, and instead of humans becoming more famous, humans shall sink lower and lower, and it shall be more and more fully perceived that it is the Lord. Little works, such as have been common in our churches for years, where twos and threes are added, are quite consistent with great self-congratulation, and so is utter barrenness; mark the pompous carriage of many a fruitless preacher and see if it is not so. Let the Lord make bare His arm and the person humbles himself in the dust, for when hundreds are ingathered, this cannot be the minister, this is the finger of God. The human being is forgotten, then, in the very abundance of his success, and the Lord alone is magnified in that day. Oh, that God would do in the churches of England some great and stupendous works by all His ministers! Then would they discover their own weakness, and then would the name of God be glorified. You frequently meet with the observation, if someone is successful in winning souls, "I am afraid he will grow proud: how we ought to pray that he may be kept humble!" That is a very necessary prayer for anybody; but it is no more necessary for the person who is successful than for the unsuccessful one; in fact, it is an assumption of pride on any person's part to think that he has less need to pray against pride than any other man or woman. Think not that when the church prospers it becomes necessarily proud. No, the very fullness of the boat makes it sink, and the very abundance of the miracle makes us cry out the more, "It is the Lord," for we feel that it could not have been of human beings, for it is out of human reach to have accomplished such wonders.

So far, then, there is a likeness running through the whole. Means must be used; means alone, unavailing; Christ's presence gives the success; that success develops human weakness and leads to the exclamation—"It is the Lord."

Remarking the Dissimilarity

Allow us to say in the commencement that we think the first picture represents the church of God as we see it; the second represents it as it really is. The first pictures to us the visible, the second the invisible. Luke tells us what the crowd sees; John tells us what Christ showed to His disciples alone. The first is common truth which the multitude may receive, the next is special mystery revealed only to spiritual minds. Observe, then, carefully, the points of divergence.

First, there is a difference in the orders given. In the first, it is, "Launch out into the deep, and let down your nets for a draught." In the second it is, "Cast the net on the right side of the ship." The first is Christ's order to every minister; the second is the secret work of His Spirit in the word. The first shows us that the ministry is to fish anywhere and everywhere. All the orders that the Christian has as to his preaching is, "Launch out into the deep and let down your net." He is not to single out any particular character; he is to preach to everybody, sensible sinners and insensible sinners. He is to preach to the dead dry bones of the valley as well as to the living souls. He is not to look where the fish are, but just to throw the net in, doing as his Master tells him. "Go ye into all the world, and preach the gospel to every creature." Those ministers who preach only to the elect should remember this. Our business is to include all sorts of fish, and not to be particular about where we are, but just splash the net in. What if we are in town, or city, or village? What if we are among the rich or poor, learned or illiterate? What if we are among the debauched or immoral? We have nothing to do with that—our duty is the same, to "launch out into the deep, and let down the net"—that is all. Christ will find the fish: it is no business of ours. The secret truth is that when we are doing this the Lord knows how to guide us so that we "cast the net on the right side of the ship." That is the secret and invisible work of the Spirit, whereby He so adapts our ministry, which is in itself general, that He makes it particular and special. We speak to all, and He speaks to some. We blow the trumpet, but only the bankrupt debtors hear it. Only those who are truly of the Spirit of God know the joyful sound and rejoice therein. We cannot single them out, but God can. We thrust in the blessed lodestone of the Gospel, and that heavenly magnet has an affinity to some hearts that God has quickened, so that as many as were ordained to eternal life believe. The apostles preached to the crowd, but the Lord God the Holy Spirit, who had decreed the salvation of His chosen, sent the word home with power to the chosen and separated ones. What a joy it is to think that we always have a picked congregation here, for the Lord has picked them! Though they are crowded together indiscriminately—here the good and there the bad, all sorts mingled and mixed together—yet God brings them in according to His eternal purpose, and all the while there is a core of chosen souls inside the mass of the congregation to whom God is applying the word. We cast the net, after all, on the right side of the ship, and we do find it full.

In the first instance you will clearly see that there is a distinct plurality. The fishermen have nets—in the plural; they have boats—in the plural. There is plurality of agency employed. Each man seems to come out distinctly. In the next case, it is one. There are many men, but they are all in *one boat*. They unitedly drag the net, and it is but *one net*—there is no division, it is all one. Now, this is the visible and the invisible. To us, the means that God makes use of to bring sinners to Himself are various. Sometimes we are in one boat trying to catch all the fish we can. There is another boat over yonder, and they are trying to do the same. We ought to consider them as being partners, and whenever our boat gets too full, we should beckon to our partners in the other ship to come and help us. We ought not to look upon those Christians who differ from us as though they were emptying the sea, and rivaling us. The more the merrier. The more people to do good, the more will the Lord's name be praised. I think in many of our towns where some of our whining friends say that all good people should go to one chapel, that it is far better to have three or four. I question whether the plurality of agency involved in denominations is not a great boon and blessing. Instead of in the slightest degree standing out against other Christians for carrying out their convictions, praise them and look upon them as partners in another ship. Our denominational distinctions help to keep us awake, thus we stir one another up, and do far more good in the world than would be the case if there were only a nominal church. God would have the agency diverse. There must be several nets, and there must be several fishermen, and these fishermen in different boats. So far as we are able to see, there will always be a Paul and a Barnabas who cannot get on together; there will always be outward divisions in the ministry; I avow myself the advocate and

The Two Draughts of Fishes 119

lover of these things. As I said last Sabbath, the thing called Sectarianism I do not disown but maintain.

But let us look to the inward. In John 21 they are all in one boat, all fishing together, all dragging one net. Ah, brethren, this is what is really the fact. We do not see it, but all God's ministers are dragging one net, and all God's church is in one ship. Oh, I bless God for that sweet doctrine! It is no use striving after outward uniformity; we shall never see it. Neither the texture of the human mind nor the will of God require it. It is of no use to contend against the diversities which exist in the great visible church; I do not know that these differences are evils. They are the natural results of human finite character, and must and will exist to the end of the chapter. It is the unity of the Spirit; it is unity in Christ Jesus; it is unity in love to one another that God would have us regard. Let us learn this unity from the fact that after all, though we may look as if we differed, yet if we are God's ministers, there is only one ministry; if we are God's church, there is only one church in the world; there is only one spouse of the Lord Jesus; there is only one fold and one shepherd. Though to our eyes it will always be so, two boats, or twenty boats; two nets, ay, fifty nets, yet to Him who sees all things better than we do, there is only one boat and one net; they shall all who are taken in that one net be safely brought to shore.

Thirdly, there is another difference. In the first case, how many fish were caught? The text says, "a great multitude." In the second case, a great multitude are taken too, but they are all counted and numbered. "A hundred and fifty and three." Luke does not tell us how many were caught the first time, for there were some of them not worth the counting; but the second time you will perceive the exact number is recorded, "a hundred and fifty and three." What was *Peter's* reason for counting them? We cannot tell. But I think I know why the Lord made him do it. It was to show us that though the number of the saved is to us a matter of which we know nothing definitely, yet secretly and invisibly the Lord has counted them even to the odd one; He knows well how many the Gospel net shall bring in. See where the Word is preached what a great multitude are brought in! Thousands, tens of thousands are added to the different churches of Christ, and make a profession of their faith. It were impossible to reckon all over Christendom how many have been taken in the outward net of the visible church of Christ. But it is quite possible for it to be known of God how many shall be brought at last, and how many now are in the *invisible* church. He has counted them, foreordained their number, fixed them, settled them. The number one hundred fifty-three seems to me to represent a large definite number. They shall be in heaven a number that no one can number, for God's elect are not few; but they shall be a number whom God can number, for "the Lord knoweth them that are his." They shall be a number certain and fixed, which shall neither be diminished nor increased, but shall abide the same according to His purpose and will. Now, *I*, as a preacher, have nothing to do with counting fish. My business is with the great multitude. Splash goes the net again! Oh, Master! You who have taught us to throw the net and bring in a multitude, guide into it the hundred and fifty and three!

Yet again, notice another difference. The fish that were taken the first time appear to have been of all sorts. The net was broken, and therefore, doubtless some of them got out again; there were some so little that they were not worth eating, and doubtless were thrown away. "They shall gather the good into vessels and throw the bad away." In the second case, the net was full of great fishes; they were all great fishes, all good for eating, all the one hundred fifty-three were worth the keeping, there was not one little fellow to be thrown back into the deep again. The first gives us the outward and visible effect of the ministry. We gather into Christ's church a great number. And there will always be in that number some that are not good, that are not really called of God. Sometimes we have church meetings in which we have to throw the bad away. We have many blissful meetings where it is gathering in the fish—and what big hauls of fish has God given to us! Glory be to His name! But at other times we have to sit down and tell our fish over, and there are some who must be thrown away; neither God nor human can endure them. Thus is it in the outward and visible church. Let no one be surprised if the tares grow up with the wheat—it is the order of things, it must be so. Let none of us wonder if there are wolves in sheep's clothing—it always will be so. There was a Judas among the Twelve; there will be deceivers among us to the end of the age. Not so the invisible church—the church within the church—the Holy of Holies within the temple. In that there is none to throw away. No; the Lord who brought them into the net brought the right sort in. He did not bring one hypocrite or apostate; having brought them in to the exact number of one hundred fifty-three, they cannot one of them get out again, but they are kept in that net, for that net does not break. They are in the secret, invisible church of Christ, and they cannot get out of it, let them do what they may. They may even give up their nominal profession, and thus get out of the visible church, but they cannot give up their secret possession. They cannot escape from the secret and invisible church, and they shall all be kept there until the net is dragged to land, and the whole hundred fifty-three saved.

Yet again, you notice in the first case the net broke, and in the second case it did not. Now, in the first case, in the visible church the net breaks. My brethren are always calling out "the net is broken!" No doubt it is a bad thing for nets to break; but you need not wonder at it. We cannot just now, when the net is full, stop to mend it; it will break. It is the necessary consequence of our being what we are that the net will break. What do I mean by this? Why, that instead of having some one denomination, we have twenty or thirty! The net is broken. I do not at all grieve over it. I believe it is what must be as long as we are flesh and blood. For until you get a set of perfect people, you never will have anything but these divisions. The net must break and will break. But glory be to God, the net does not break, after all, in reality, for though the visible church may seem to be rent and torn to pieces, the invisible church is one. God's chosen, God's called, God's quickened, God's blood-bought—they are one in heart, and one in soul, and one in spirit. Though they may wear different names among humans, yet they still wear, before God, their Father's name written on their foreheads; they are and always must be one

You perceive, brethren, that I do not advise you to strive after a nominal unity. The more you strive after that, the more divisions there will be. Certain people left many of our denominations and formed, they said, a church that would not be a sect. All they did was to make a sect the most sectarian of sects—the most narrow and most bitter of cliques, though containing some of the best men and women, some of the best Christians, and the ablest writers of the times. You cannot make a visible uniformity, it is beyond your power—the net is broken. There now! Take care of the fish and leave the net alone, but still maintain the unity of the Spirit in the bond of perfectness. Take care that you are not a schismatic in your heart, that you hold no heresy in your soul, that you are one with all them that love the Lord Jesus Christ in sincerity, and in this you will soon see that the net is not broken, but that the saints are one. Ah, I bless God that when we get with God's people—it does not matter what they are—we soon find the net is not broken. There is many a godly clergyman of the church of England with whom I commune with the greatest joy, and I have found the net was not broken. In conversing with Christians of all denominations, some who from doctrine, some who from sentiment stand wide as the poles asunder, I have still found and known that there was such a real and perfect harmony of heart that the net was not broken. I do not believe that charity would ever have had such perfect work in Christ's church if it had not been for our being divided into tribes, like the twelve tribes of old. It is no charity for me to love another who thinks as I think—I cannot very well help it. But for me to love a dear brother or sister who differs from me in some points, why there is exercise and room for my charity; as God has left trials and troubles to exercise faith, I believe He has left us in many doctrinal difficulties on purpose to exercise our love until the day shall come when we shall all grow to the stature of perfect men and women in Christ Jesus. The net is not broken, friends; do not believe it, and when you read about this denomination and that do not be grieved at these names and tribes, but rather thank God for them. Say, that is the visible church, and the net is broken, but there is an invisible church where the net is not broken, where we are one in Christ and must be one forever.

There are several other points of difference, but I think we have hardly time to enlarge upon them. I will only hint at them. In the first case, which is the visible church, you see the human weakness becomes the strongest point; there is the boat ready to sink, there is the net broken, there are the men all out of heart, frightened, amazed, and begging the Master to go away. In the other case it is not so at all. There is human weakness, but still they are made strong enough. They have no strength to spare, as you perceive, but still they are strong enough, the net does not break, the ship goes slowly to land dragging the fish; and then, lastly, Simon Peter pulls the fish to shore. Strong he must have been. They were just strong enough to get their fish to shore. So in the visible church of Christ you will often have to mourn over human weakness: but in the invisible church, God will make His servants just strong enough—just strong enough to drag their fish to shore. The agencies, means, instrumentalities shall have just sufficient force to land every elect soul in heaven, that God may be glorified.

Then, notice, in the first case, in the visible church they launched out into the deep. In the second case, it says they were not far from the shore, but a little way. So today our preaching seems to us to be going out into the great stormy deep after fish. We appear to have a long way to reach before we shall bring these precious souls to land. But in the sight of God we are not far from shore; when a soul is saved, he or she is not far from heaven. To us there are years of temptation, and trial, and conflict; but to God, the Most High, it is finished—"it is done." They are saved: they are not far from shore.

In the first case, the disciples had to forsake all and follow Christ. In the second, they sat down to feast with Him at the dainty banquet which He had spread. So in the visible church today we have to bear trial and self-denial for Christ, but glory be to God, the eye of faith perceives that we shall soon drag our net to land, and then the Master will say, "Come and dine." We shall sit down and feast in His presence, with Abraham, Isaac, and Jacob, in the kingdom of God.

One Among Many Lessons Which the Two Narratives in Common Seem to Teach

In the first case, Christ was in the ship. Oh, blessed be God, Christ is in His church, though she launch out into the deep. In the second case,

The Two Draughts of Fishes 123

Christ was on the shore. Blessed be God, Christ is in heaven. He is not here, but He has risen; He has gone up on high for us. But whether He is in the church, or whether He is on the shore in heaven, *all our night's toiling shall, by His presence, have a rich reward.* That is the lesson. Mother, will you learn it? You have been toiling long for your children. It has been night with you as yet. They give no evidence of grace; rather they give many signs of sin, and they grieve your spirit. Your night's toiling shall have an end; you shall at last cast the net on the right side of the ship. Sunday school teacher, you have been diligently laboring long, and with but little fruit. Be not discouraged, the Master will not let you work in vain; in due season you shall reap if you faint not. As these disciples had a great sea harvest, so shall you have a harvest of souls. Minister, you have been plowing some barren rock, and as yet no joyful sheaves have made your heart glad. You shall, doubtless, "Come again, rejoicing, bringing your sheaves with you." And you, O church of God, travailing for souls, meeting daily in prayer, pleading with people that they will come to Christ, what if they are not saved yet? The morning comes, the night is far spent, and the Master Himself shall soon appear; though He may not find faith on the earth, yet His advent shall bring to His church the success for which she has waited—such success that as a woman remembers no more her travail because a child is born into the world, so shall the church remember no more her toils, her efforts and her prayers, because Christ's kingdom has come, and His will is done on earth even as it is in heaven. Work, dear friends! If there are any of you that are not working, *begin now*; if there are any of you not saved as yet, the Lord grant that when the Word is preached, you may be caught in it as in a net. We do throw it out once this morning; we hope to throw it again this evening. "Believe in the Lord Jesus Christ, and thou shalt be saved," for "he that believeth and is baptized shall be saved, and he that believeth not shall be damned." Flee to Christ! Escape from the wrath to come! May the Spirit apply that word to you, and lead you to the place where high on Calvary with bleeding hands and feet the Savior died! One look at Him and you are saved. Look, sinner, and live! God save you, for Christ's sake! Amen.

10

Good Cheer from Grace Received

And, behold, a woman, which was diseased with an issue of blood twelve years, came behind him, and touched the hem of his garment: For she said within herself, If I may but touch his garment, I shall be whole. But Jesus turned him about, and when he saw her, he said, Daughter, be of good comfort; thy faith hath made thee whole. And the woman was made whole from that hour (Matt. 9:20–22).

But as he went the people thronged him. And a woman having an issue of blood twelve years, which had spent all her living upon physicians, neither could be healed of any, came behind him, and touched the border of his garment: and immediately her issue of blood stanched. And Jesus said, Who touched me? When all denied, Peter and they that were him said, Master, the multitude throng thee and press thee, and sayest thou, Who touched me? And Jesus said, Somebody hath touched me: for I perceive that virtue is gone out of me. And when the woman saw that she was not hid, she came trembling, and falling down before him, she declared unto him before all the people for what cause she had touched him, and how she was healed immediately. And he said unto her, Daughter, be of good comfort: thy faith had made thee whole; go in peace (Luke 8:42–48).

The words of good cheer which our Savior spoke to this woman were not given to her while she was coming to Him, for that would have been premature. She had not avowed her desire to be healed, she had uttered no prayer, she had actually as yet sought nothing at the Savior's hands and, hence, she had not reached the stage at which comfort is fitting. She does not appear to have required comfort in taking

---

This sermon was taken from *The Metropolitan Tabernacle Pulpit* and was preached at the Metropolitan Tabernacle, Newington.

her first step; she was resolved upon that, she took it without fail. It is one of the unwisest things under heaven to comfort people who do not require it. When we are dealing with inquirers, our love may bring them loss if we offer them words of cheer when they need admonition or rebuke. Any comfort which keeps a soul short of Christ is dangerous. A sinner's main business is to get to Jesus Himself, to exercise personal faith in the personal savior; we have no right to a gleam of comfort until we have heartily and honestly trusted in Christ. If encouragements to believe are used as a sort of halfway house to rest in before actually believing, they are mischievously used, and may ruin our souls.

This afflicted woman did not require to be cheered so soon for she had such confidence in Christ, and such a resolve to put her confidence to the test, that difficulties could not hinder her, nor crowds keep her back. The Savior was in the press, she joined the throng, and with a holy boldness mixed with a sacred modesty she came behind Him, only wishing to touch His garment, or even the fringe of it, feeling persuaded that if she did but come into contact with the Lord, no matter how, she would be healed. According to her faith so was it done to her, and *it was after she had been healed that our Lord spoke comfortingly to her*. He brought not forth the cup of cordial until the need for it had fully come. After she had touched Him and her faith had made her whole, a trial awaited her, and her spirit was ready to faint, and then the tender One cheered her by saying, "Thy faith hath made thee whole; go in peace."

It happens to many and many a heart that after it has obtained the blessing of salvation and has been healed of the disease of sin, a time of fear occurs. After it has made its confession of faith, a season of trembling follows, occurring, perhaps, as a reaction from the joy of salvation, a rebound of the spirit from excessive delight. We eat the heavenly provision eagerly, and it is sweet to our taste; yet, afterward, our long hunger having weakened us, we do not digest the food with ease, and pains ensue for which medicine is required. We fear and tremble because of the greatness of the mercy received, and then this word is wanted: "Be of good comfort: thy faith hath made thee whole."

We will meditate, first, upon *this woman's need of comfort*; secondly, upon *the comfort which Jesus gave her*; and then, in the third place, we will enter a little further into that comfort, and think of *the faith which Jesus Christ declared had made her whole*—the faith to which He pointed her for comfort.

The Woman's Need of Good Cheer

Come, then, dear friend, and attentively consider this woman's need of good cheer. She felt in her body that she was made whole, and yet she stood in urgent need of comfort. This necessity arose from several causes.

First, *she had hoped to obtain the blessing secretly, and she was found out.* She thought that by coming behind the Lord Jesus in the press she would not be observed, and she anxiously desired secrecy because the peculiarity of her bodily disorder caused her to dread publicity. She aimed at gaining her end and retreating unnoticed into the multitude. Truth to tell, she stole the cure. Her touch was given in stealth, no eye resting upon her. No disciple seems to have spied her out, nor had anyone in the throng perceived the deed, or else, when the Master said, "Who touched me?" one or other of them would have pointed her out. So far, she had shunned observation, and even the Savior Himself had not seen her with His bodily eyes; but faith such as hers could not be hid. It was not meet that such a flower should bloom unseen. She is called for, and she stands discovered, the center of all eyes.

You, perhaps, dear friend, have hoped to find salvation and to keep it a secret. You entered the house of prayer a stranger to the things of God, but very anxious. There you sat and wept, but you tried to conceal your feelings from those who sat near you. You have gone in and out of the place of worship seeking the Savior, but fearing to be suspected of doing so. Nobody spoke to you, or, if anyone did, you evaded all the questions that were put to you, for you were as jealous of your secret as if you carried diamonds and were afraid of thieves.

Now you have believed in the Savior, or at least you hope so, but you court secrecy just as much. You have found honey, and you have tried to eat it all alone, not because you grudge others sharing it with you, but because you are afraid of them. You did not wish mother or father, kinsfolk or acquaintance to suspect you of being a Christian; you shrank from the blessed charge and desired to be a secret friend of Jesus, a Nicodemus, or a Joseph of Arimathea. To your great amazement, you have been found out. Like Saul, you hid among the stuff, but the people have called you forth. Your love to Jesus has oozed out, and is spoken of by many. Do you wonder? How can fire be hidden? Your speech has betrayed you. Your manner and spirit have discovered you, as odors betray sweet flowers. And now that it is out, you feel a sinking of spirit at the notice you have attracted. Your modesty cries, "They take me for a Christian. Can I live like a Christian? Shall I be able to adorn my profession? They have discovered me in the family; my brothers and sisters see that there is a change in me. Is it a real change? Or shall I turn out to be one of those deceivers who have a name to live, and yet are dead?" Your heart fails you for fear of future backsliding and apostasy; well it may, for flesh is weak, and the world is bewitching, and Satan is subtle, and sin is deceitful. Whatever comfort there is in our present meditation will be meant for you, since it is intended for persons embarrassed by being forced out of the shade of solitude into the glare of observation, troubled because they fear that they shall not honor the holy name which is named upon them. To you who are in that condition, Jesus says, at this moment, "Be of good comfort: thy faith hath made thee whole."

This poor woman, in addition to being found out, *had been constrained to make a public personal testimony.* As we have already noticed, her case was a very special one in which privacy would naturally be courted. But that privacy had been invaded, the Savior had looked for her and had demanded, "Who touched me?" and she, all trembling and afraid, had been constrained to fall down before Him, and to tell Him all the truth. Do you wonder that the excitement was too much for her? The people had been astonished as they heard of the wondrous power which had emanated from the person of Christ, even through the fringe of His garment, and that astonishment in a great measure referred to her. She was the observed of all observers. Of her cure she had to make a public acknowledgment. She was equal to the task. Being brought to bay, she did her work bravely, and bore full and telling testimony. Take careful note that our Lord did not bid her be of good cheer until she had so done. She trembled before she confessed the Lord's deed of grace which had worked upon her; but, as soon as she had made a public avowal, her Lord said to her, "Daughter, be of good comfort."

I have known certain timid ones who have wished to unite with the church on the sly and to make no open confession either by word of mouth or by baptism. I have refused to be a party to the breeding of cowards, and they have lived to thank me for what seemed a harsh demand. Yet, when the confession has been made once for all, many brave hearts have been full of anxiety and downcastings. They have confessed Christ before other people, they have told out what the Lord has done for their souls; and after it has been all over, they have been overwhelmed with a sense of responsibility, and have said within themselves, "What great things will be expected of me! What have I had the courage to say? Shall I be able to live up to it all?" After the bold, open confession comes the inward shrinking, though they are not sorry that they made the avowal, for, on the contrary, they would make it a thousand times over if they could glorify Christ thereby. Yet they know their weakness, and tremble lest they should ever behave themselves so as to prove unworthy of the cause of their beloved Redeemer. If you, dear friend, have just come out from the world, and have newly said, "I am on the Lord's side," do not feel surprise if what you have just done should, upon calm consideration, look almost like presumption.

A sense of fear is natural when you see to what a service your dedication vows have bound you. At such a time, Jesus will give you the comfort of the text, "Be of good cheer; thy faith hath made thee whole." May you have grace to receive it by faith, and to drink in all its consolation!

This, however, is not quite all the reason for the woman's needing encouragement at the moment the Lord bestowed it. This woman, no doubt, *had a very deep reverence for the Lord Jesus Christ.* She had such an esteem for Him that even His garments were thought by her to be saturated with healing energy; when she found herself immediately in His presence, she trembled and was afraid. She had come behind Him, no doubt, to a great extent out of modesty and humility as well as out of timidity. Now she finds herself face-to-face with the glorious Lord, and He is asking her questions, and in full view of all the people she has to avow her faith in Him. I hardly think that she was afraid of the people, but I do think that her faith was so reverential that she felt an awe at being found immediately in the presence of the Lord.

Beloved friend, you have been singing lately—

> Happy day, happy day,
> When Jesus washed my sins away.

You have joined in meetings where all have been filled with a sacred delight because they have met with Jesus; I should not wonder if, when you have been at home afterward alone and you have thought the matter over, it has seemed too gracious a thing to be really true that the Lord of glory had lovingly communed with you. As your thoughts of Him have risen in reverential love, you have said, "Is it possible? Is it true! Am I not dreaming? Has the Son of God really looked on me in love? Can it be true that He, who wears the majesty of heaven, has set His heart upon me, and has come to tabernacle in my breast? This is a miracle of miracles! Is it indeed a fact?" You have felt pressed down by the weight of the divine goodness. I remember well, not only the joy I had when I found the Savior, but the horror of great darkness which fell upon me within a very short time after I had rejoiced with joy unspeakable. It was on this account: I knew that I had found the Lord. I was fully assured of my salvation, and full of joy as to my possession of His love. But then I asked, "Is it not too good to be true! Is salvation altogether of free grace? Is there an everlasting love of God and is it fixed on me? Am I indeed an heir of God, and a joint-heir with Jesus Christ?" The brightness of the glory blinded my weak eyes; by floods of amazing love I was carried off my feet. Are you in such a condition? Then it is time for the Savior's gentle words to sound in your heart, "Be of good comfort: thy faith hath made thee whole." When a reverent sense of the Lord's amazing condescension causes us to swoon at heart, He will stay us with flagons, and comfort us with apples. This is a sweet melancholy which infinite love can soon relieve. Perhaps, the greatest reason for the trembling of the woman in the narrative lay in *a sense of her faulty coming*. When she looked back at the way in which she had approached the Lord, she saw a mass of faults in it, as we may well do in ours. When she had been made whole, her faith would say to her, "The blessed Lord did not deserve that you should come behind Him, and touch His garment in that *unbelieving* fashion. See what a Savior He is! What love, what tenderness shines in His face! Why did you not come to Him openly? You crouched in the rear; why did you not look Him full in the face, and crave His mercy? He would have received you freely, why did you suspect His grace? You may have wounded Him by doubting His willingness to bless you. You should not have indulged such unbelief." After a seeker has found the Lord, and has experienced salvation, he is sometimes tempted to question whether he is really a believer in Jesus. He reasons within himself thus—"My faith is so mixed with unbelief that I am ashamed of it. Why did I come to Jesus in such a way as I did come? Oh, that I had come in a more childlike spirit, and that I had done Him the justice to have a greater confidence in Him!" Do you, dear friend, know this experience? If so, to you and to all others who are thus exercised, the comfort of our text is addressed.

Very likely, conscience would charge the trembling woman with a dishonest *stealth* in her way of getting her cure. "You felt, at the time, that you had no right to the blessing; but you snatched at it, and did not ask the Savior's leave to take it. You thought that you would be healed, and then run away, and none would be any the wiser; thus you robbed the Lord of His glory. Can a blessing rest on such a way of acting?" Conscience made her tremble; therefore, the Savior as good as said, "Daughter, do not suspect your faith, for it has made you whole, and therefore it is good faith. However it acted, it has brought you healing, therefore do not distress yourself about its imperfections, but go in peace." He pointed her for comfort to the fact that, however faulty might be the way of her coming, it had healed her, and therefore she might well be content. Is there not a word of cheer in this for us also? If we have been renewed in heart and life, the faith by which this change was wrought cannot but be good.

Perhaps, too, she might have felt that it was sadly *too bold* of her, a woman unclean according to the law, to push among the throng, and dare to touch the Lord Himself. Many and many a time my heart has whispered to itself, "How could you be so bold as to trust Christ?" The Devil has called it presumption, and my trembling heart has feared it might be so. One thing I know, I am certain that I am healed, even as the woman knew that the cure was wrought in her. This I do know, that I am not what I once was, but I am made a new creature in Christ Jesus. Yet the question will propose itself, "How can it be that you dared to dash in and seize on mercy, being such a sinner and so utterly unworthy?"

For my own part, I confess that I acted toward the Lord Jesus somewhat like a poor starving dog who saw meat in the butcher's shop and could not restrain himself from laying hold thereon and running away with it. Many a butcher would chase such a wretched creature and take the meat from him; but our Savior is of a nobler temper. If our Lord Jesus sees us grasp His mercy, He will never take it away from us. He says, "Him that cometh to me I will in no wise cast out." O you who are quite unfit to come to Christ and altogether unworthy of His favor, you are the very people who may come, and welcome! O you who say that you have no warrant to come to Jesus, He would have you come without any warrant but His own Word, which says, "Whosoever will, let him come." Let your want of inward warrant be your warrant; you are needy and sinful, be this your passport. Come along with you and boldly grasp the covenanted mercy. It will not be theft, for Jesus has already given over Himself and all that He has to all who are willing to have Him. Have courage to take freely what the Lord freely gives.

> To sinners poor, like me and you,
> He saith he'll "freely give";
> Come, thirsty souls, and prove it's true;
> Drink, and forever live.

Yet it may be that, after you have done so, and after you have obtained the blessing, you will fall into a fainting fit, and swoon with fear because you question your own right to it. Hearken to a word of comfort. "Possession is nine points of the law," and it is all the ten points of the Gospel. So long as you have Christ, there is no need to ask how you got Him. Yet the trembling conscience whispers, "You had no right to believe. You are not the person who should have ventured to trust in Jesus." Then you will need a cheering word, and then will you have it, even as our dear Master said, "Daughter, be of good comfort; thy faith hath made thee whole." Let what grace has done for you plead your justification for having believed in Jesus. If you are indeed changed and renewed, question not your faith, but believe yet more, and you shall see greater things than these.

Thus, then, I set forth the woman's need of comfort, and if anyone else is in a like case to hers, let him look up and be of good cheer, for other feet have walked the way of fear before Him. Let him say, as Augustus Toplady did—

> If my Lord himself reveal,
> No other good I want;
> Only Christ my wounds can heal,
> Or silence my complaint.
>
> He that suffer'd in my stead,
> Shall my physician be;
> I will not be comforted
> Until Jesus comforts me.

The Comfort Which Jesus Gave Her

May the Holy Spirit rest upon us while we notice the comfort which Jesus gave her. He said to her, "Daughter, be of good comfort; thy faith hath made thee whole."

There was comfort in the loving title. To call her "daughter" was most kind and tender. I suppose that she must have been of much the same age as our Lord Himself, and therefore He did not call her "daughter" because of her youth. When our Lord said "daughter," He expressed His tender consideration for her, which made Him feel toward her as tenderly as a father to a child. *Sister* would have been the word, if He had only meant human relationship, but *daughter* meant careful affection. While Jesus is our Brother, there is a sense in which He is our Father also, and He exercises toward His poor, downcast children a father's pity and care.

Such a title must have dispelled her fears. To be so near of kin to Him who had wrought a matchless cure upon her was consolation enough. Let our tried and cast-down friends rest with us concerning this matter: you have believed in Jesus and you have confessed His name and you are made whole; go your way in peace. Henceforth you belong to Christ, and you are related to Christ as His daughter or son; do not, therefore, question your right, since the grace of adoption has confirmed it. If the Lord calls you His daughter, you did no wrong when you touched your Father's garment. If He avows you as His child, be not so unwise as to question the divine declaration. Your rights and privileges henceforth are almost boundless. You may do much more than touch His garment's hem, you may lean on His breast. He gives you greater privileges than those which you have yet enjoyed, yes, favors beyond what you ask or even think. To those who believe on Him, He gives the right and privilege "to become the sons of God, even to them that believe on his name," so that all question about your right to do this or that may be ended, for He calls you His own beloved child, and says, "Be of good comfort."

The main point of consolation was that she was cured: Jesus said to her, "Thy faith hath made thee whole," which would bring her comfort in several ways. First, *it was a great consolation that her impurity was gone.* So, my brother and sister, if you have believed in Jesus, you are no longer regarded as unclean before the Lord. The blood of the Lord Jesus has removed your defilement. You are "accepted in the Beloved"; His blood, like the hyssop of which David sang, has purged you, and you are clean. Do not look upon yourself as being what you are not, but know yourself to be whiter than snow in Christ Jesus. In the removal of your guilt and the renewal of your nature, the source of your defilement is destroyed. Do not, therefore, hide your face and stand afar off from God, but come boldly to the throne of grace, since grace has made you meet to come. When, my anxious friend, you come before the Lord with the recollection of all your past transgressions, you may well be ashamed and confounded, and feel as if you could never open your mouth anymore. But know of a surety that your sins have ceased to be, they shall not be mentioned against you anymore forever: God, even the God of judgment, has blotted out the record. Humble yourself for having been a transgressor, but let a sense of perfect forgiveness embolden you in coming to your Savior.

Whatever you once were, God views you not as you were in yourself, but as what you are in Christ Jesus. When you come to His table and feast among His family, do not hesitate to feel at home, although it cannot be denied that you once stood at the swine trough and hungered after husks. Say within your believing on my hand, and shoes on my feet, therefore I will eat and drink as He bids me, and I will not mar the music and the merriment He had received me safe and sound, and shall I not be glad at being thus received?" God be thanked, that, though you were the servants of sin, you have obeyed from the heart that form of doctrine which was delivered to you, and you are now brought into the glorious liberty of the children of God. Though you were once unclean, polluted, and polluting, it may be said of you, "but ye are washed, but ye are sanctified." Perhaps your old name will stick to you as theirs did to Rahab the harlot, and to Simon the leper; but do not feel degraded, since the Lord has turned away your reproach. Hear Jesus Christ Himself say to you, "Daughter, be of good comfort; thy faith hath made thee whole."

Remember that and rejoice in His presence. You have a right to be among His people, for your faith has made you whole, and this is the mark which all His people wear. You are a sinner, it is true; but you are a sinner saved from wrath through infinite love. You are no longer a miserable sinner, and why should you call yourself so? You are a happy, blessed, forgiven child whom the Lord has taken from the dunghill and set among His princely children. Rejoice, therefore,

Good Cheer from Grace Received

because your faith has made you whole. Is this not a theme for boundless gratitude? Come boldly into the church; come boldly to the throne of grace; for you are so cleansed by the blood of atonement that you may come unquestioned even into the Holy of Holies. Has not Jesus said, "He that is washed is clean every whit"?

The woman was comforted by being made to see in her cure that Jesus was not angry with her: Our Lord, in effect, said to the saved woman, "Have you been afraid that you did wrong in touching Me? Are you fearful lest I should be grieved because you did not believe enough in Me to come and face Me, but must steal behind Me? Do you suspect that I shall blame you because of the littleness of your faith? Now"— He puts it so sweetly—"do not think so, but be of good comfort, for your faith has made you whole." Though her faith dared only to touch the hem of His garment, it was evidently acceptable faith for because of it the Lord had made her whole. It is clear that the Lord has not rejected our faith when He owns and honors it. He cannot be vexed at a confidence which He has evidently rewarded.

Beloved friend, has your faith been such that it has made you abhor sin? Has it been such that the things you once loved you now hate, and the things you once hated you now love? Has your faith made a complete change in you? Are you a new person in Christ Jesus? Have you been made whole morally and spiritually? Then, be sure that no wrong faith could have wrought this good work in you; a faith that produces wholeness or holiness of life cannot have been a mistake. Whether in your coming to Jesus you came behind Him or before Him, whether you touched His gracious hand or touched His garment's hem, whether you did it secretly or did it publicly, all these inquiries are interesting, but not essential. For if a change of heart has been wrought in you and you are saved, then the Lord Jesus must be pleased with you. He could not have wrought a great work in you and yet be angry with you. Therefore, you need not be troubled as to the way in which you came to Him. "Be of good comfort; thy faith hath made thee whole," is a most sweet and effectual way of lulling fears to rest.

Possibly, the poor woman may have been haunted by the fear that she would suffer a relapse, but our Lord consoles her by *the assurance that her faith had effectually made her whole*. She had not obtained a little time of deliverance from the evil, so that it would recur, but she was made whole. The Lord gives her a medical certificate; He sends her forth with a clean bill of health. Oh, how sweet it is when Jesus Christ gives to any one of us a full assurance of complete salvation, so that we are delivered from all fear of the malady's return and can walk abroad free from fear! I know that some Christians think that after Christ has saved us and given us new hearts, the old hearts may come back; and though His grace is in us a well of water which He promises shall spring up to everlasting life, yet they think that it may dry up to the last drop. Beloved, I do not thus read the Word, but the very opposite is clear to me in Sacred Writ. The work of God in the soul is a lasting and an everlasting work; if you are once healed by Christ, He has wrought in you an effectual cure which will hold good throughout time and throughout eternity. Solomon truly said, "I know that, whatsoever God doeth, it shall be forever." He who has made you whole will keep you whole, for His gifts and calling are without repentance.

The comfort to the woman in the narrative was meant, as we have seen, to meet the trial occasioned by her open confession. She had been driven to reveal her secret, and this to a large extent caused her trembling. She would rather have hidden in the press, but she was called to the front, and made to confess Jesus before all. The Savior, in effect, says, "You need not be ashamed to tell your story, for *it ends well*, since you are made whole. You need not be ashamed to let everybody know that your faith has healed you; what does it matter what your sickness was, if you are now recovered from it?" It will be no disgrace to us to confess our guilt if, at the same moment, we are assured of full forgiveness. It is annoying to hear persons talk flippantly of their sins before conversion as though they were proud of them. They seem to glory in them as a Greenwich pensioner might boast of his battles and his broken bones; such things are to be mentioned with blushes and tears. Say as little as you can about those things whereof you are now ashamed, and let what you do say be spoken in lowliest penitence. Still, there are times when you are bound to tell out your case to the praise of the glory of the grace which so abounded where your sin abounded. Then you need not be afraid to tell your story, for grace has made it end so well. Let the world know that, though foully defiled, you came into contact with the Savior by simply, humbly believing in Him, and that by this simple means you are saved.

Once more, if anyone is conscious that faith has saved him, he may take to himself the good cheer of the text and use it wherever he goes, *for nothing can happen to him so bad as that which has been removed.* "Thy faith has saved thee," is an antidote for many ills. "I am very poor," says one; so was this woman, for she had spent all that she had upon physicians; but Jesus said to her, "Thy faith hath made thee whole." I am very sick," cries a friend, "I feel low and ill"; but "thy faith hath *saved* thee"; is not this joy enough? Oh, what a blessing it is to be saved! That you are saved is enough to set all your nature ablaze with joy. I am sure that the healed woman felt rich, though she had not two cents to chink together in her pocket; she was made whole by faith, and that was wealth enough for her. To be one of the Lord's saved ones is joy enough to upbear the heart under every affliction.

Do you not see that if your faith has changed your character and delivered you from the desperate plague of sin, there remains no longer any impossibility or even difficulty in the way of duty? You have been half afraid to try to teach the children in the Sunday school; but surely, since your faith has made you whole, you can teach a few little children! You have been afraid to address a score of people in a village chapel; but you need not be afraid to try if God has called you, for the faith which has made you whole can give you "a word in season." What is there that faith cannot do? Why, if my faith has had the power to drop the burden of my sin into the sepulcher of my Lord, what is there that it cannot accomplish? If, by that faith, my soul has risen from among the dead, and taken its seat at the right hand of the Father in the heavenly places in Christ, what shall stand in its way? If we have to force a passage through a throng of devils, we need not hesitate; though all the world combine and stand against us, we need not fear. Our faith has made us whole; who can undo the miracle? A faith which by divine grace saves us from hell and secures us for heaven, what is there that it cannot accomplish? It laughs at impossibilities and marches from strength to strength in majestic serenity. Holy confidence shall win victory upon victory until at last it shall cry, "I have fought a good fight, I have finished my course, I have kept the faith; henceforth there is laid up for me a crown of righteousness, which the Lord, the righteous Judge, shall give me at that day." I cannot imagine a sweeter consolation than this: "Thy faith hath made thee whole; go in peace"; endeavor to suck the honey out of it.

The Faith Which Our Lord Commended

It made her whole; that is its best certificate of excellence. There is much to note in reference to that faith, but a few brief hints may suffice. Her faith is to be commended because *it outlived a long season of discouragement.* She had been twelve years afflicted—think of that! Patience had indeed had its perfect work in her. But she believed in Christ for a cure and the cure came to her. So will it be with everyone who will believe in Jesus. If there could be a soul found which had been living in sin twelve hundred years, if it had faith in Jesus, He would make it whole. After half a century of impenitence, he that believes in Christ Jesus is saved at once. Eighty years of sin vanish in a moment when a man or woman trusts in the great atonement. Come, dear unconverted friend, and cast yourself at Christ's feet at this quiet hour, for He will not cast you out.

The faith which healed this poor woman had *survived many failures*; she had been deceived by all sorts of quacks and medicine men, and yet she had not lost the capacity for faith. It is said that she had "suffered many things of many physicians," and I can well believe it, for if you read the prescriptions of the old doctors you will quite agree that poor humanity has suffered many things from "the faculty." The way in which the ancient doctors went to work to cure their patients much resembled that which someone would follow who was eager to kill them. Dr. Sangrado, by his bleeding and drenching, has sent many into a premature grave; and in Christ's time, if you wanted to be well the first rule was to avoid all physicians.

I will tell you the names of a few spiritual doctors to whom I beseech you not to go, for if you do you will suffer a great deal from them, but get no good. There is one whose name is Dr. Self-confidence, who is in partnership with a relative called Dr. Self-righteousness. Dr. Legality, and his son Mr. Civility, are another popular pair of cheats. You will find them at home whenever you call, and they will give you bitter doses or silver-coated pills as they see fit, but never a whit the better will you be. There is a doctor about just now who was educated by the Jesuits, and practices the Romeopathic system—wafers and wine-and-water are his specific; to this school belong Mr. Surgeon Ceremonies and Doctor Sacraments. None of these can heal a sick soul. Have nothing to do with them, but apply to the beloved Physician, even the Lord Jesus Christ. Some of us went around to most of these pretenders and gave them a long trial; though we were disappointed in them all, yet we still were enabled to believe in Jesus Christ. Dear friend, do the same. Though you have been disappointed everywhere else, yet go and knock at Christ's door, and that faith of yours, which leaps over discouragement, will make you whole.

Her faith *believed in simple touching*; she used no ceremonies, she only believed. It was a faith which believed that she would be healed *without payment*. She took the cure gratis; she offered no fee. That is Gospel faith which takes Christ's forgiveness without money and without price, just as He presents it in the Gospel. Hers was a great faith, for she believed that Christ could heal her *when He was occupied with healing another*. He was hastening to the house of Jairus to work a miracle there, and yet she believed that He could heal her on the way. Can you, dear reader, believe in this fashion? Do you know, of a surety, that however Jesus may be now occupied, He can without difficulty at this moment pardon and save you? If you have reached so great a confidence, then give the saving touch and trust Him once for all.

The poor sick soul had a faith which assured her that *Christ could bless her when His back was turned*. Can you also reach this point?

Good Cheer from Grace Received

Some of God's own children can hardly trust Him when they see the light of His countenance, but this woman could trust Him when His back was turned toward her. I would to God that we had, each of us, such confidence in Jesus that we would not doubt under any circumstances His power and willingness to save all who trust Him. He must save those who rely upon Him. It is a necessity of His nature that those who touch Him should receive healing from Him.

Trusting in Jesus is a person's best evidence that he is saved, for it is written, "He that believeth in him is not condemned." Faith has made its possessor whole, whoever he may be; if you are resting alone in Jesus and His finished work, the life of the holy has begun in you, and you may therefore "be of good comfort."

11
A Sabbath Miracle

And he was teaching in one of the synagogues on the sabbath. And, behold, there was a woman which had a spirit of infirmity eighteen years, and was bowed together, and could in no wise lift up herself. And when Jesus saw her, he called her to him, and said unto her, Woman, thou art loosed from thine infirmity. And he laid his hands on her: and immediately she was made straight, and glorified God (Luke 13:10–13).

What blessed days Sabbath days are! I mean not only the Jewish Sabbath on the seventh day of the week, but the Christian Sabbath on the first day of the week. I remember a friend in Newcastle telling me that when he was looking at a house in that city which was to be let, he was taken to the top of it, and the agent said to him, "You see that there is a fine view from here. You can see a long way today; but, on Sundays, you can see Durham Cathedral." My friend asked, "Why on Sundays?" The reply was, "You cannot see it all the rest of the week because of the smoke; but, on Sundays, it is usually clear enough to get a glimpse of it." What views some of us have had of heaven, and what views of Jesus Christ have been accorded to us on Sabbath days! We might have seen Him on other days if there had not been so much smoke from business, and care, and sin; but the blessed breath from heaven has blown it all away on the Lord's Day, and we have been able to look even into that which is within the veil.

Our Lord Jesus Christ has performed wonders of grace on all the days of the week. I would not be surprised to hear that there are Christians here who were converted on a Monday, or a Tuesday, or a Wednesday, or a Thursday, or a Friday, or a Saturday; but I would quite expect to learn that for everyone of them there are ten here who were

---

This sermon was taken from *The Metropolitan Tabernacle Pulpit* and was preached on Sunday evening, June 11, 1876.

brought to Christ on the Sabbath. Heaven's gates seem to be set more widely open on that day than during the rest of the week, or else we have more inclination to enter them then. When the full history of the Sabbath shall be unfolded, we shall begin to know what infinite mercy it was on God's part to set aside one day in seven especially for His worship and for our spiritual benefit. Thousands upon thousands, yes, millions upon millions have found Jesus very near, and rejoiced in Him on the Lord's Day.

Our Savior was wont to use the day for public worship and for the pursuance of His high and holy calling of blessing the children of men. So, finding that on that day He could meet with many in the synagogue, He was accustomed to go there, and to teach. Among the people who came on the particular Sabbath of which our text speaks, there was one poor woman who was possessed by an evil spirit, and that evil spirit had, I suppose, so affected her nerves, and so influenced her entire system, that her spinal cord was greatly weakened. Evidently, she had suffered from the worst kind of curvature of the spine, for she was bent double, "and could in no wise lift up herself." I am afraid that if any one of you had been in such a sad state as that, you would have said, "I shall never go to the synagogue any more"; and that your friends would have said, "We think you had better not go. You are such an object, and you are so unwell, that you will be best at home. You can read a good book there, and you can worship God just as acceptably in your own parlor as you can by going up to the public assembly of His people." I am also afraid that there are some here who would have felt that they could be excused for a much lighter affliction than that poor woman suffered from, for I have known some who could not come out to the service if it happened to be wet, though they went to business on wet days. Many people imagine that Sunday is a convenient day for being ill and getting a little rest, so as to be fortified for the more important business which requires all their energies upon the Monday and during the rest of the week. It seems as though they thought that cheating God out of His day is a very small matter, but that robbing themselves of even a portion of a day would greatly grieve them.

If this poor woman had not gone to the synagogue, I do not know that she would ever have met with Christ; so I commend her example to you, even if your bodily infirmities increase so much that you might make very justifiable excuses for being absent. There was a dear sister, now in heaven, who attended this Tabernacle for years, though she was so deaf that she never heard a word that was spoken. The reasons she gave for being here were that, at any rate, she could join in the hymns, and that, had she stayed away, she would have felt as if she was dissociated from the people of God. Other people, perhaps, might not have known the reason for her absence, and it might, therefore, have been a bad example to them. So she said, "Though I do not hear a word, I love to be there"; and she has told me that some of the happiest hours she has ever spent have been those when she has thus had communion with the people of God, although she could not fully understand all that was being said or done. In like manner, dear friends, as often as the people of God assemble for worship, come with them.

Notice one thing more about this woman. She did not get any good through going to the synagogue, so long as she merely went there. She went to the synagogue bent double; and she came back bent double. If she went all those eighteen years, as I daresay she did, she was unable to lift up herself all that long time. Do not, I pray you—you who are regular attendants at the house of God, and yet remain unsaved—get into the notion that all you need is to attend divine service so many times on the Sabbath day or on week nights; for if you do, you will not be likely ever to get a blessing. This poor woman was not healed until she met with the Lord Jesus Christ, and I wish each one of you would come here saying, "Oh, that I might meet with Jesus today! Oh, that Jesus would meet with me!" It is a rule, with very few exceptions, that what a person fishes for he is most likely to catch. If any come here merely out of idle curiosity, it is possible, though not certain, that their curiosity will be satisfied; if any come to find fault, I have no doubt that they will find plenty to complain of; but if any of you have come determined to find Christ if He is to be found, it will be a very surprising thing if you have to go away without discovering Him. This is what you really need if you are to be restored from all the ills that sin has wrought, you must come to Christ Himself.

Christ's Compassion Was Excited

Jesus, while He was teaching in the synagogue, looked into the faces of His congregation; and, as He looked at them, He saw this woman, and His heart was at once moved with compassion toward her.

Note that *it was not her prayers that moved Him*, or any plea she urged, for she did not speak to Him, or plead with Him. This was one of the cases in which no request for healing was presented to the Savior; it was the sight of her misery that touched His heart. Perhaps, dear friends, if she had not been bent double, Christ's notice might not have been so quickly drawn to her; but because she was what people call "quite an object," and looked so sad, she attracted Christ's attention.

Notice, also, that *Christ was not moved to compassion by the prayers of anybody else for her*. Sometimes, He healed the sick when their fathers, or mothers, or friends brought them to Him; but nobody brought this poor woman to Jesus. It does not seem as if anybody had

A Sabbath Miracle

sufficient compassion upon her to ask Jesus to heal her; or, if they had the compassion, they had not enough faith to believe that it was possible for her to be healed. There she was, a poor lone woman; and, possibly, it was the sight of her, with not a friend to help her, that touched Christ's heart and moved Him to fix His gaze upon her with a view to curing her sad complaint.

Notice, further, that *Christ's heart was not touched by any description which she gave Him of her condition.* She gave Him no description and none was needed. He looked at her; that was all that was required, for He already knew all about her. She did not say, "I have been bound by Satan for eighteen years"; but Christ knew that she had been. As He looked at her, He read her life story, as someone reads a book; and as He read the story, His heart was moved with compassion toward her. I wonder whether there is a soul here that has not been asking the Lord for a blessing because that soul does not think it is likely that any blessing would come. I wonder whether there is anyone here who has not dared to hope, and therefore has not dared to pray. My Master has a wonderful eye for such souls as these. There may have been in that synagogue a man wearing a gold ring or a woman in a fine dress, but Christ did not notice them or their adornment. He picked out the person who was the most miserable, the most wretched, and who most needed His pity. Upon her He fixed those blessed eyes of His with a compassion tender as the heart of a woman, and His whole soul was moved with pity for her because she was so grievously bound by the accursed power of Satan.

Now let us look at this woman's case a little more closely. She "was bowed together, and could in no wise lift up herself." That, in itself, was a painful thing; all the beauty of the woman's form and figure had gone, but being bent double like that must have produced most serious injury to every organ of the poor creature's body. I have no doubt that she was the subject of a thousand aches and pains through the posture in which she had been bent. Besides, it is a beautiful thing to be able to look up; but to be always obliged to look down is something terrible. Through this trying affliction, the poor woman could not even see the Savior, though, happily, He could see her, bent down as she was in the crowd. Instead of looking up with the face of a woman, she had to carry her head down toward the earth like a poor beast, and I should not wonder if the spirit of evil that was in her had made her feel unhappy, sorrowful, and almost despairing. I am also inclined to think that her mind may have been, like her body, bent toward the earth, and that this, too, was caused by satanic influence. Perhaps the worst point about her case was that she had been for eighteen years in that sad condition. We do not know how it came about. She may, as a girl, have run in the fields, and have spent her days right merrily; but, on a sudden, perhaps, there came upon her this evil spirit, and she began to feel weakness of the spine. By and by, she was bent double, the sun of her life was put out, and her days were dark with sorrow and pain; this had continued for eighteen years! What a long time that is to be such a sufferer! Eighteen years of happiness may pass very quickly, but eighteen years of pain is a very long period. This woman, for eighteen years could not lift up her head to look at the sun; for eighteen years Satan had possessed her and had bowed her body together and had filled her mind with morbid thoughts and dreary dreams and terrible forebodings of dreadful things to happen in the future. Jesus knew all about those eighteen years, so we do not wonder that He had compassion upon her.

Possibly, in this congregation—no, I am quite sure I have some who in soul are like this poor woman was in body. You feel that you would gladly give all you have to be saved, but you have long ago given up all hope of that. You did, at one time, hear the gospel with some degree of pleasure; but now, even while you listen to it, you keep on condemning yourself, and saying, "Salvation will never come to me." You have fallen into a condition of chronic melancholy; you are so sad that friends, who used to cheer you, give you up in despair. Perhaps they call you foolish; God knows that it is not folly, but a most grievous calamity that has happened to you. You cannot see Jesus, and you do not think that He can see you, but He does, and that is the only ray of hope for you. If I were to attempt to comfort you, I know that I would fail. If you are the person of whom I am thinking, no language from merely human lips will ever comfort you; there will have to be a divine voice reaching your inmost soul, or else you never will be loosed from your infirmity. We meet with some such persons every now and then, and we try to cheer them; it is right that we should do so. We pity them, and we are quite sure that our Lord Jesus Christ pities them still more, for there is not one of us whose heart is one half so tender toward his fellowman as the heart of Christ Himself is and must be. So, you poor afflicted one, tossed with tempest, and not comforted—you downtrodden, sin-burdened soul, Jesus picks you out of this throng, as He picked out that poor woman in the synagogue, that He may have mercy upon you as He had upon her.

Jesus Issued a Command: "He called her to him."

Somehow or other, He managed to attract her attention; then, probably not without considerable difficulty and pain, she made a great effort, and, at last was able to see Him; He said something to this effect, "Will that poor woman, over yonder, who is bent double, come here to Me?" Whatever words He may have used, we know that "he called her to him." Was not that command *a proof of great grace and condescension*

A Sabbath Miracle

on Christ's part? If He, the Messiah, who spoke as never man spoke, had called the ruler of the synagogue, and spoken familiarly to him, one might not have wondered so much. Yet, out of all that throng, He did not call anyone except that poor, decrepit, bowed-down, Satan-possessed daughter of Abraham; we are expressly told that "he called her to him." He might have called to her from a distance, and said "Be healed," but He did not, for He wished to show His special sympathy with such a sad case of suffering.

This call was not only given in great condescension, but it was also *given directly and personally to her*: "he called *her* to him." If Jesus had said, "I wish any person here, who suffers from a spirit of infirmity, to come to Me," perhaps she might have come, perhaps she might not; but, instead of giving a general intimation like that, He fixed His eye on her, and "called her to him." Do any of you recollect a sermon—I do very well—in which the preacher seemed to speak to nobody but yourself? I am fully persuaded that if I had been like the prisoners in some of our jails, shut up in a box where I could not see anybody but the preacher—on the occasion when the Lord met with me, the preacher could not have addressed himself more pointedly to me than he then did. On the occasion to which our text refers, Christ addressed Himself to this woman personally and pointedly. I am hoping that the description I have given of the woman will make someone here say, "Ah, that is just my case!" Well, if so, O poor bowed-down daughter, poor languishing, desponding man, Jesus calls you! If that description applies to you, take the personal call to yourself, and say, "This condescending, pointed call is addressed to me."

Then do as this poor woman did; make it *a call which was promptly obeyed.* I daresay that the other people in the synagogue were very surprised that Christ called *her*, yet they made way for her, and—strange object as she was—perhaps, every step painful to her—she managed to get where Christ was. As she was coming toward Him, she heard Him make this extraordinary statement, "Woman, thou art loosed from thine infirmity"; and when she got close to Him, He laid both His hands on her, "and immediately she was made straight." How startled she must have been—even at Christ's first call—and little did she dream that He was going to cure her in such a fashion. Perhaps there is someone here whom Christ means to save, yet you have not even been thinking of Him. Nevertheless, thus is it written in the counsels of eternity, "In the Tabernacle, on that summer Sunday night, such-and-such a soul must be delivered from the bondage of Satan." If it is so written, all the devils in hell cannot hold you captive beyond the appointed moment; all the weight of your sins, and the evil habits that you have formed and so long practiced, shall burn like so much tow in a blazing fire, for God's eternal decree of mercy must be fulfilled. He who comes to deliver you is none other than Christ, the Son of God, "mighty to save," before whom gates of brass are broken and bars of iron are snapped in two. It was a glorious Sabbath for that poor woman when the Lord came forth determined to heal her, and this will be a glorious Sabbath for you if the Lord now resolves to save you. He is even now calling you doubters, you desponding ones, you who have given up all hope; He is calling *you*, will you not come to Him? Will you not trust Him? He asks you to believe, not that you are good, but that He is good—not that you can be healed by your neighbor, but that you can be healed by your Savior. He asks you to come and listen to His gracious words while He says, "Thy sins are forgiven thee; go in peace." "I have blotted out, as a thick cloud, thy transgressions, and, as a cloud, thy sins: return unto me, for I have redeemed thee."

Christ's Power Was Manifested

Jesus said to her, "*Woman, thou art loosed from thine infirmity.*" It is the Word of the Lord that has power in it. Whenever people are converted, and brought to Christ, it is by God's Word that the deed is done. Fine sermons never win souls; you may blaze away, young man, at a terrific rate, with your brilliant oratory, and your fine pieces of poetry and questions from eminent authors, and your peroration may be like the set piece at a display of fireworks, or the final burst of brightness with which it all ends, but all that will not save souls. What does save souls, then? Why, the Word of the Lord, the truth as it is in Jesus. I have noticed that the very words of Scripture are usually those that reach the heart. So, brethren and sisters, if you really want to find the Lord, give good heed to His Word; incline your ear and come to Him; hear, and your soul shall live; for "faith cometh by hearing, and hearing by the Word of God."

In addition to speaking to the woman, Christ laid His hands on her; and that is the way that healing reaches sin-sick souls, by being brought into contact with Christ. When the pure humanity of Christ is recognized by us and we perceive that He is our Brother and our Friend—when we see that He bears both our sins and our sorrows, and carries our sicknesses in His own blessed Person—when we realize that Christ has become our Representative and Surety—a sense of peace comes to our souls. One reason why Jesus is so well qualified to save us is that—

> He knows what sore temptations mean,
> For he has felt the same.

He is, therefore, able to succor them that are tempted. Bowed-down woman, He puts His pierced hands upon you. Sorely troubled man, do you not know that God has taken your nature upon Himself and now says to you, "Be comforted, for I have loved you, and lived for you, and died for you"? God grant that you may feel that healing touch, and experience that divine deliverance this very hour!

That afflicted woman was healed immediately. One of the most wonderful things about Christ's cures was that, as a general rule, they were wrought in an instant. Can you imagine—I have often tried to do so—the strange sensations that passed through some of those people when they were healed in a moment? Think of this poor woman—eighteen years bent double—and then completely restored in a single instant! What a paradise must have been condensed into those few minutes! At first, I suppose she may have thought that she was only dreaming. What! was she able to stand upright and to look into the face of Him who had wrought such a wonderful cure for her? The rapture must have seemed almost too much for her when she realized that she was healed in an instant; what if, just now, you should be saved in an instant? Remember that to pardon sin does not take God a single second; to save a soul from death and hell is a more rapid work than for the lightning's bolt to fall from heaven. At one moment, a great load of sin may be upon you, and you may be fully conscious of the terrible burden; the next instant, every sin is gone, and you are conscious that it is so, and ready to leap for joy. Nobody can work this mighty miracle of mercy but the Lord Jesus Christ; yet He can do it more swiftly than I can speak of it. Oh, that some who have been bound by Satan for eighteen years, or even longer, may prove that they do not need eighteen minutes, or even eighteen seconds to get free, but may they now look to Jesus, and believing in Him, find instantaneous healing!

Once more, *this woman's cure was perfect*, as well as instantaneous. She did not lift herself up a little and find that the satanic bondage was being somewhat relaxed; she was perfectly healed, and, better still, she was permanently healed. Her malady did not come back again. We have known doctors set a man up for a little time, and after that there has been a relapse. But this woman was both made straight and kept straight; if we believe in the Lord Jesus Christ, the salvation which He gives us, though it is instantaneous, is also perfect and everlasting, for whosoever trusts in Christ is saved immediately and saved forever. The gifts and calling of God are not matters for repentance on His part; He does not give salvation and then take it back. But having once given it, it remains the property of its possessor world without end. Then, what a precious Christ He is and what a glorious Healer! I hope some sick one here is saying, "I wish He would look this way; oh, that Jesus would look on me!" He *is* looking upon you, soul; hear what He says to you, "Come to Me, trust in Me." If you trust Jesus now, though you have been bent double these eighteen, these twenty-eight, these thirty-eight, these forty-eight, these fifty-eight, these sixty-eight—these ninety-eight years, or these hundred and eighteen years, if such a person could be—if you did but look to Him, come to Him, trust Him, in a moment He would make you whole. Oh, that you may do so!

Christ's Power Was Glorified

It is said of this woman that immediately, being made straight, she "glorified God." I should think she did. I would not mind having interruptions in our service from people who had found Christ. Our Methodist friends, in the olden times when they found peace used to shout "Hallelujah!" Well, if they really had found Christ, I think they were warranted in shouting. If ever a man might cry "Eureka! Eureka!" it was not the old philosopher, but the newborn child of God. Oh, what bliss it is to find the Savior! If one were for a little while delirious with the excessive joy of being saved by grace, it might be excusable. It is said that some of our young converts are wonderfully enthusiastic. Yes, and well they may be. If you had received such a blessing as they have, you would be enthusiastic, too. If you have ever known the weight of sin crushing you to the dust and then have had it suddenly borne away, you must have felt a mighty rebound when that great load has been removed. Could that healed woman help clapping her hands? Did she not stand up before the whole congregation in the synagogue and say, "That man must be the Son of God, blessed be His holy name! After eighteen years of bondage, He has healed me in a moment." Or suppose that she was of the very quiet sort—like most of you, good sisters—if she did not say a word, yet I think she glorified God by simply standing up straight. If she did not say anything but just walked away home, all who had known her in her long time of affliction when they saw her stand up, a fine, tall, handsome woman, and knew that she must be the same person, must have been struck with wonder, and have said, "What new power is this? Who but God could thus have restored this woman?" I would like, brothers and sisters in Christ, that you and I should so live that our very lives would preach for Jesus Christ—that people would only have to listen to our ordinary conversation, or to see the cheerfulness of our countenances, or to perceive the hopefulness of our spirits under trouble, our justness and integrity, our readiness to forgive, our zeal for God. It is good to preach with your tongue if God has called you to do so, but never forget that the best preaching in the world is done by other members of the body. So, preach with your feet—by your walk and conversation; let your whole being be a living, powerful, irresistible illustration of the power of Jesus Christ to bless and save.

A Sabbath Miracle

It was so in the case of this woman, for I do not think that, after she had clapped her hands once and stood up to testify before the whole congregation, that she had done glorifying God. Oh, no; all her life long, she would be glad to tell that story over and over again. I wonder whether she got married after that wonderful healing. It is very likely that she did; if so, and she had children of her own, as they sat on her knee, one of the first stories she would tell them would be about when she was bent double for eighteen years, and then that wonderful Prophet called her to Him in the synagogue one Sabbath day, and made her straight in a moment. Perhaps she lived long enough to tell the story of Christ's suffering and death. If she ever saw any of her grandchildren, I am sure they would say, "Come, Granny, tell us your story," and she would tell it so well that they would want to hear it again and again.

I think that every Christian should go home to his friends, and tell them what great things the Lord has done for him. There is a brother—not far from me at this moment—who had been a wild young man, fond of all the sports of the country. He went to London and heard a sermon that was the means of his conversion. When he went home one of his friends with whom he used to follow the hounds said to him, "Well, Tom, what is the best thing you heard in London?" And Tom replied, "The best thing I heard in London is that 'Christ Jesus came into the world to save sinners.'" "Oh!" said his companion, "you have gone mad." "No," answered Tom, "I was mad before I went to London, but I have gotten cured." I hope you will be able to give such testimony as that concerning what Jesus Christ has done for your souls, even as this poor woman "was made straight, and glorified God."

Some people may say to you, "You had better hold your tongue, for you will break down if you try to tell such a story as that." That would be the very best thing you could do. There is nothing like a breakdown when you are telling your story of redeeming grace and dying love. It is the very glory of it when you break down with emotion and cannot say anymore, for your hearers will be all the more anxious to know the rest of it, and there will be a deeper impression produced by your breakdown than there would have been if you had kept right on. But, anyhow, do tell the story; tell it as long as you have any breath in your body; tell how "Jesus has done all things well," and saved your soul. Make heaven and earth to ring with the glad news. When you go home to glory, tell the angels all about it, for they will be glad to hear your story, and they will break out into fresh praise as they listen to it. May God thus bless every one of you, for Jesus Christ's sake! Amen.

12
Young Man, Is This for You?

And it came to pass the day after, that he went into a city called Nain; and many of his disciples went with him, and much people. Now when he came nigh to the gate of the city, behold, there was a dead man carried out, the only son of his mother, and she was a widow: and much people of the city was with her. And when the Lord saw her, he had compassion on her, and said unto her, Weep not. And he came and touched the bier: and they that bare him stood still. And he said, Young man, I say unto thee, Arise. And he that was dead sat up, and began to speak. And he delivered him to his mother. And there came a fear on all: and they glorified God, saying, That a great prophet is risen up among us; and, That God hath visited his people. And this rumor of him went forth throughout all Judea, and throughout all the region round about (Luke 7:11–17).

Behold, dear friends, the overflowing, ever-flowing power of our Lord Jesus Christ. He had wrought a great work upon the centurion's servant, and now, only a day after, He raises the dead. "It came to pass the day after, that he went into a city called Nain." Day to day utters speech concerning His deeds of goodness. Did He save your friend yesterday? His fullness is the same; if you seek Him, His love and grace will flow to you today. He blesses this day, and He blesses the day after. Never is our divine Lord compelled to pause until He has recovered His resources, but virtue goes out of Him forever. Those thousands of years have not diminished the aboundings of His power to bless.

Behold, also, the readiness and naturalness of the outgoings of His life-giving power. Our Savior was journeying, and He works miracles while on the road: "He went into a city called Nain." It was incidentally,

---

This sermon was taken from *The Metropolitan Tabernacle Pulpit* and was preached on Sunday morning, January 15, 1888.

Young Man, Is This for You?

some would say accidentally, that He met the funeral procession; and at once He restored to life this dead young man. Our blessed Lord was not standing still, as one professionally called in. He does not seem to have come to Nain at anyone's request for the display of His love, but He was passing through the gate into the city for some reason which is not recorded. See, my brothers and sisters, how the Lord Jesus is always ready to save! He healed the woman who touched Him in the throng when He was on the road to quite another person's house. The mere spillings and droppings of the Lord's cup of grace are marvelous. Here He gives life to the dead when He is *en route*; He scatters His mercy by the roadside, and anywhere and everywhere His paths drop fatness. No time, no place, can find Jesus unwilling or unable. When Baal is on a journey, or sleeps, his deluded worshipers cannot hope for his help; but when Jesus journeys or sleeps, a word will find Him ready to conquer death or to quell the tempest.

It was a remarkable incident, this meeting of the two processions at the gates of Nain. If someone with a fine imagination could picture it, what an opportunity he would have for developing his poetical genius! I venture on no such effort. Yonder a procession descends from the city. Our spiritual eyes see death upon the pale horse coming forth from the city gate with great exultation. He has taken another captive. Upon that bier behold the spoils of the dread conqueror! Mourners by their tears confess the victory of death. Like a general riding in triumph to the Roman capitol, death bears his spoils to the tomb. What shall hinder him? Suddenly the procession is arrested by another: a company of disciples and much people are coming up the hill. We need not look at the company, but we may fix our eyes upon one who stands in the center, a man in whom lowliness was always evident, and yet majesty was never wanting. It is the living Lord, even He who only has immortality, and in Him death has now met his destroyer. The battle is short and decisive; no blows are struck, for death has already done his utmost. With a finger the chariot of death is arrested; with a word the spoil is taken from the mighty, and the lawful captive is delivered. Death flies defeated from the gates of the city, while Tabor and Hermon, which both looked down upon the scene, rejoice in the name of the Lord. This was a rehearsal upon a small scale of that which shall happen by and by, when those who are in their graves shall hear the voice of the Son of God and live; then shall the last enemy be destroyed. Only let death come into contact with Him who is our life and it is compelled to relax its hold, whatever may be the spoil which it has captured. Soon shall our Lord come in His glory, and then before the gates of the New Jerusalem we shall see the miracle at the gates of Nain multiplied a myriad times.

Thus, you see, our subject would naturally conduct us to the doctrine of the resurrection of the dead, which is one of the foundation stones of our most holy faith. That grand truth I have often declared to you, and will do so again and again; but at this time I have selected my text for a very practical purpose which concerns the souls of some for whom I am greatly anxious. The narrative before us records a fact, a literal fact, but the record may be used for spiritual instruction. All our Lord's miracles were intended to be parables; they were intended to instruct as well as to impress; they are sermons to the eye, just as His spoken discourses were sermons to the ear. We see here how Jesus can deal with spiritual death, and how He can impart spiritual life at His pleasure. Oh, that we may see this done this morning in the midst of this great assembly!

The Spiritually Dead Cause Great Grief to Their Gracious Friends

If an ungodly individual is favored to have Christian relatives, he causes them much anxiety. As a natural fact, this dead young man who was being carried out to his burial caused his mother's heart to burst with grief. She showed by her tears that her heart was overflowing with sorrow. The Savior said to her, "Weep not," because he saw how deeply she was troubled. Many of my dear young friends may be deeply thankful that they have friends who are grieving over them. It is a sad thing that your conduct should grieve them, but it is a hopeful circumstance for you that you have those around you who do thus grieve. If all approved of your evil ways you would no doubt continue in them, and go speedily to destruction; but it is a blessing that arresting voices do at least a little hinder you. Besides, it may yet be that our Lord will listen to the silent oratory of your mother's tears and that this morning He may bless you for her sake. See how the Evangelist puts it: "When the Lord saw *her*, he had compassion on *her*, and said unto *her*, Weep not." And then he said to the young man, "Arise."

Many young persons who are in some respects amiable and hopeful nevertheless, being spiritually dead *are causing great sorrow to those who love them best*. It would perhaps be honest to say that they do not intend to inflict all this sorrow; indeed, they think it quite unnecessary. Yet they are a daily burden to those whom they love. Their conduct is such that when it is thought over in the silence of a mother's chamber, she cannot help but weep. Her son went with her to the house of God when he was a boy, but now he finds his pleasure in a very different quarter. Being beyond all control now, the young man does not choose to go with his mother. She would not wish to deprive him of his liberty, but she laments that he exercises that liberty so unwisely. She mourns that he has not the inclination to hear the Word of the Lord and become a servant of his mother's God. She had hoped that he would follow in his father's footsteps and unite with the people of God, but he takes quite the opposite course. She has seen a good deal about him lately which has deepened her anxiety: he is forming companionships and other connections which are sadly harmful to him; he has a distaste for the quietude of home; he has been exhibiting to his mother a spirit which wounds her. It may be that what he has said and done is not meant to be unkind, but it is very grievous to the heart that watches over him so tenderly. She sees a growing indifference to everything that is good, and an unconcealed intention to see the vicious side of life. She knows a little, and fears more, as to his present state, and she dreads that he will go from one sin to another until he ruins himself for this life and the next.

O friends, it is to a gracious heart a very great grief to have an unconverted child, and yet more so if that child is a mother's boy, her only boy, and she a desolate woman from whom her husband has been snatched away. To see spiritual death rampant in one so dear is a sore sorrow which causes many a mother to mourn in secret and pour out her soul before God. Many a Hannah has become a woman of a sorrowful spirit through her own child. How sad that he who should have made her the gladdest among women has filled her life with bitterness! Many a mother has had so to grieve over her son as almost to cry, "Would God he had never been born!" It is so in thousands of cases. If it be so in your case, dear friend, take home my words to yourself and reflect upon them.

The cause of grief lies here: *we mourn that they should be in such a case*. In the story before us the mother wept because her son was dead; we sorrow because our young friends are spiritually dead. There is a life infinitely higher than the life which quickens our material bodies, and oh, that all of you knew it! You who are unrenewed do not know anything about this true life. Oh, how we wish you did! It seems to us a dreadful thing that you should be dead to God, dead to Christ, dead to the Holy Spirit. It is sad indeed that you should be dead to those divine truths which are the delight and strength of our souls, dead to those holy motives which keep us back from evil and spur us on to virtue, dead to those sacred joys which often bring us very near the gates of heaven. We cannot look at a dead man and feel joy in him, whoever he may be; a corpse, however delicately dressed, is a sad sight. We cannot look upon you, you poor dead souls, without crying out, "O God, shall it always be so? Shall not these dry bones live? Will You not quicken them?" The apostle speaks of one who lived in pleasure, and he said of her, "She is dead while she liveth." Numbers of persons are dead in reference to all that is truest and noblest, and most divine, and yet in ether respects they are full of life and activity. Oh, to think that they should be dead to God, and yet so full of jollity and energy! Marvel not that we grieve about them.

We also mourn because we lose the help and comfort which they ought to bring us. This widowed mother no doubt mourned her boy not only because he was dead, but because in him she had lost her earthly stay. She must have regarded him as the staff of her age and the comfort of her loneliness. "She was a *widow.*" I question if anybody but a widow understands the full sorrow of that word. We may put ourselves by sympathy into the position of one who has lost her other self, the partner of her life; but the tenderest sympathy cannot fully realize the actual cleavage of bereavement and the desolation of love's loss. "She was a widow"—the sentence sounds like a knell. Still, if the sun of her life was gone, there was a star shining; she had a boy, a dear boy, who promised her great comfort. He would no doubt supply her necessities and cheer her loneliness, and in him her husband would live again and his name would remain among the living in Israel. She could lean on him as she went to the synagogue; she would have him to come home from his work at evening and to keep the little home together and to cheer her hearth. Alas! that star is swallowed up in the darkness. He is dead, and today he is born to the cemetery. It is the same spiritually with us in reference to our unconverted friends. With regard to you that are dead in sin, we feel that we miss the aid and comfort which we ought to receive from you in our service of the living God. We want fresh laborers in all sorts of places—in our Sunday school work, in our mission among the masses, and in all manner of service for the Lord we love! Ours is a gigantic burden, and we long for our sons and daughters to put their shoulders to it. We did look forward to see you grow up in the fear of God and stand side by side with us in the great warfare against evil and in holy labor for the Lord Jesus; but you cannot help us, for you are yourselves on the wrong side. Alas, alas! you hinder us by causing the world to say, "See how those young people are acting!" We have to spend thought, and prayer and effort over you which might usefully have gone forth for others. Our care for yonder great dark world which lies all around us is very pressing, but you do not share it with us. People are perishing from lack of knowledge and you do not help us in endeavoring to enlighten them.

A further grief is that we can have no fellowship with them. The mother at Nain could have no communion with her dear son now that he was dead, for the dead know not anything. He can never speak to her, nor she to him, for he is on the bier, "a dead man carried out." O my friends, certain of you have dear ones whom you love, and they love you; but they cannot hold any spiritual communion with you, nor you with them. You never bow the knee together in private prayer, nor mingle heart with heart in the appeal of faith to God as to the cares which prowl around your home. O young man, when your mother's heart leaps for joy because of the love of Christ shed abroad in her soul, you cannot understand her joy. Her feelings are a mystery to you. If you are a dutiful son, you do not say anything disrespectful about her religion, but yet you cannot sympathize in its sorrows or its joys. Between your mother and you there is upon the best things a gulf as wide as if you were actually dead on the bier, and she stood weeping over your corpse. I remember in the hour of overwhelming anguish when I feared that my beloved wife was about to be taken from me, how I was comforted by the loving prayers of my two dear sons. We had communion not only in our grief, but in our confidence in the living God. We knelt together and poured out our hearts to God, and we were comforted. How I blessed God that I had in my children such sweet support! But suppose they had been ungodly young men! I would have looked in vain for holy fellowship and for aid at the throne of grace. Alas! in many a household the mother cannot have communion with her own son and daughter on that point which is most vital and enduring because they are spiritually dead, while she has been quickened into newness of life by the Holy Spirit.

Moreover, *spiritual death soon produces manifest causes for sorrow.* In the narrative before us the time had come when her son's body must be buried. She could not wish to have that dead form longer in the home with her. It is a token to us of the terrible power of death that it conquers love with regard to the body. Abraham loved his Sarah, but after a while he had to say to the sons of Heth, "Give me a possession of a buryingplace with you, that I may bury my dead out of my sight." It happens in some mournful cases that character becomes so bad that no comfort in life can be enjoyed while the erring one is within the home circle. We have known parents who have felt that they could not have their son at home, so drunken, so debauched had he become. Not always wisely, yet sometimes almost of necessity, the plan has been tried of sending the incorrigible youth to a distant colony in the hope that when removed from pernicious influences he might do better. How seldom so deplorable an experiment succeeds! I have known mothers who would not think of their children without feeling pangs far more bitter than those they endured at their births. Woe, woe to him who causes such heartbreak!

What an awful thing it is when love's best hopes gradually die down into despair, and loving desires at last put on mourning and turn from prayers of hope to tears of regret! Words of admonition call forth such passion and blasphemy that prudence almost silences them. Then have we before us the dead young man carried out to his grave. A sorrowful voice sobs out, "He is given unto idols, let him alone." Am I addressing one whose life is now preying upon the tender heart of her that brought him forth? Do I speak to one whose outward conduct has at last become so avowedly wicked that he is a daily death to those who gave him life?

O young man, young woman, can you bear to think of this? Are you turned to stone? I cannot yet believe that you contemplate your parents' heartbreak without bitter feelings. God forbid that you should!

We also mourn because of the future of people dead in sin. This mother, whose son had already gone so far in death that he must be buried out of sight, had the further knowledge that something worse would befall him in the sepulcher to which he was being carried. It was impossible for her to think calmly of the corruption which surely follows at the heels of death. When we think of what will become of you who refuse the Lord Christ we are appalled. "After death the judgment." We could more readily go into details as to a putrid corpse than we could survey the state of a soul lost forever. We dare not linger at the mouth of hell, but we are forced to remind you that there is a place "where their worm dieth not, and the fire is not quenched." There is a place where those must abide who are driven from the presence of the Lord and from the glory of His power. It is an unendurable thought that you should be "cast into the lake of fire, which is the second death." I do not wonder that those who are not honest with you are afraid to tell you so, and that you try yourself to doubt it; but with the Bible in your hand, and a conscience in your bosom, you cannot but fear the worst if you remain apart from Jesus and the life He freely gives. If you continue as you are and persevere in your sin and unbelief to the end of life, there is no help for it but that you must be condemned in the day of judgment. The most solemn declarations of the Word of God assure you that "he that believeth not shall be damned." It is heartbreaking work to think that this should be the case with any one of you. You prattled at your mother's knee and kissed her cheek with rapturous love; why, then, will you be divided from her forever? Your father hoped that you would take his place in the church of God; how is it that you do not even care to follow him to heaven? Remember, the day comes when "one shall be taken, and the other left." Do you renounce all hope of being with your wife, your sister, your mother, at the right hand of God? You cannot wish them to go down to hell with you; have you no desire to go to heaven with them? "Come, ye blessed," will be the voice of Jesus to those who imitated their gracious Savior; "Depart from me, ye cursed, into everlasting fire, prepared for the devil and his angels," must be the sentence upon all who refuse to be made like the Lord. Why will you take your part and lot with accursed ones?

I do not know whether you find it easy to hear me this morning. I find it very hard to speak to you because my lips are not able to express my heart's feelings. Oh, that I had the forceful utterance of an Isaiah or the passionate lamentations of a Jeremiah with which to arouse your affections and your fears! Still, the Holy Spirit can use even me, and I beseech Him so to do. It is enough. I am sure you see that the spiritually dead cause great grief to those of their family who are spiritually alive.

For Such Grief There Is Only One Helper—But There Is a Helper

This young man is taken out to be buried; but *our Lord Jesus Christ met the funeral procession.* Carefully note the "coincidences," as skeptics call them, but as we call them "providences" of Scripture." This is a fine subject for another time. Take this one case. How came it that the young man died just then? How came it that this exact hour was selected for his burial? Perhaps because it was evening; but even that might not fix the precise moment. Why did the Savior that day arrange to travel twenty-five miles, so as to arrive at Nain in the evening? How came it to pass that He happened just then to be coming from a quarter which naturally led Him to enter at that particular gate from which the dead would be borne? See, He ascends the hill to the little city at the same moment when the head of the procession is coming out of the gate! He meets the dead man before the place of burial is reached. A little later and he would have been buried; a little earlier and he would have been at home lying in the darkened room, and no one might have called the Lord's attention to him. The Lord knows how to arrange all things; His forecasts are true to the tick of the clock. I hope some great purpose is to be fulfilled this morning. I do not know why you, my friend, came in here on a day when I am discoursing on this particular subject. You did not think to come, perhaps, but here you are. And Jesus has come here too; He has come here on purpose to meet you and quicken you to newness of life. There is no chance about it, eternal decrees have arranged it all, and we shall soon see that it is so. You being spiritually dead are met by Him in whom is life eternal.

The blessed Savior saw all at a glance. Out of that procession He singled out the chief mourner and read her inmost heart. He was always tender to mothers. He fixed His eye on that widow, for He knew that she was such without being informed of the fact. The dead man is her only son. He perceives all the details and feels them all intensely. Nothing is hid from His infinite mind. Your mother's heart and yours are both open to him. O young man, young woman, Jesus knows all about you. Jesus, who is invisibly present this morning, fixes His eyes on you at this moment. He has seen the tears of those who have wept for you. He sees that some of them despair of you, and are in their great grief acting like mourners at your funeral.

Jesus saw it all, and, what was more, *entered into it all.* Oh, how we ought to love our Lord that He takes such notice of our griefs, and especially our spiritual griefs about the souls of others! You, dear teacher, want your class saved: Jesus sympathizes with you. You, dear friend, have been very earnest to win souls. Know that in all this you are workers together with God. Jesus knows all about our travail of soul, and He is at one with us therein. Our travail is only His own travail rehearsed in us, according to our humble measure. When Jesus enters into our work it cannot fail. Enter, O Lord, into my work at this hour, I pray You, and bless this feeble word to my hearers! I know that hundreds of believers are saying, "Amen." How this cheers me!

Our Lord proved how He entered into the sorrowful state of things by first saying to the widow, "Weep not." At this moment He says to you who are praying and agonizing for souls, "Do not despair! Sorrow not as those who are without hope! I mean to bless you. You shall yet rejoice over life given to the dead." Let us take heart and dismiss all unbelieving fear.

Our Lord then went to the bier, and just laid His finger upon it, and *they that bare it stood still of their own accord.* Our Lord has a way of making bearers stand still without a word. Perhaps today yonder young person is being carried further into sin by the four bearers—natural passions, infidelity, bad company, and love of strong drink. It may be that pleasure and pride, willfulness and wickedness are bearing the four corners of the bier; but our Lord can, by His mysterious power, make the bearers stand still. Evil influences have become powerless, the person knows not how.

When they stood quite still, *there was a hush.* The disciples stood around the Lord, the mourners surrounded the widow, and the two crowds faced each other. There was a little space, and Jesus and the dead man were in the center. The widow pushed away her veil, and gazing through her tears wondered what was coming. The Jews who came out of the city halted as the bearers had done. Hush! Hush! What will He do? In that deep silence the Lord heard the unspoken prayers of that widow woman. I doubt not that her soul began to whisper, half in hope, and half in fear—"Oh, that He would raise my son!" At any rate, Jesus heard the flutter of the wings of desire if not of faith. Surely her eyes were speaking as she gazed on Jesus, who had so suddenly appeared. Here let us be as quiet as the scene before us. Let us be hushed for a minute and pray God to raise dead souls at this time. [Here followed a pause, much silent prayer, and many tears.]

Jesus Is Able to Work the Miracle of Life-Giving

That hush was not long, for speedily the Great Quickener entered upon His gracious work. Jesus Christ has life in Himself, and He quickens whom He will (see John 5:21). Such life is there in Him that "he that liveth and believeth in him, though he were dead, yet shall he

Young Man, Is This for You?

live." Our blessed Lord immediately went up to the bier. What lay before Him? It was a corpse. *He could derive no aid from that lifeless form.* The spectators were sure that the man was dead, for they were carrying him out to bury him. No deception was possible, for his own mother believed him dead, and you may be sure that if there had been a spark of life in him she would not have given him up to the jaws of the grave. There was then no hope—no hope from the dead man, no hope from anyone in the crowd either of bearers or of disciples. They were all powerless alike. Even so, you, O sinner, cannot save yourself, neither can any of us, or all of us, save you.

There is no help for you, dead sinner, beneath yon skies; no help in yourself or in those who love you best. But, lo, the Lord has laid help on one that is mighty. If Jesus wants the least help you cannot render it for you are dead in sins. There you lie, dead on the bier, and nothing but the sovereign power of divine omnipotence can put heavenly life into you. Your help must come from above.

While the bier stood still, Jesus spoke to the dead young man, *spoke to him personally*: "Young man, I say unto thee, Arise." O Master, personally speak to some young man this morning; or, if You will, speak to the old, or speak to a woman; but speak the word home to them. We mind not where the Lord's voice may fall. Oh, that it would now call those around me, for I feel that there are dead ones all over the building! I stand with biers all about me, and dead ones on them. Lord Jesus, are You not here? What is wanted is Your personal call. Speak, Lord, we beseech You!

"Young man," said He, "arise"; and *He spoke as if the man had been alive.* This is the Gospel way. He did not wait until He saw signs of life before He bade him rise, but to the dead man He said, "Arise." This is the model of Gospel preaching: in the name of the Lord Jesus, His commissioned servants speak to the dead as if they were alive. Some of my brethren cavil at this and say that it is inconsistent and foolish, but all through the New Testament it is even so. There we read, "Arise from the dead, and Christ shall give thee light." I do not attempt to justify it; it is more than enough for me that so I read the Word of God. We are to bid men and women believe on the Lord Jesus Christ even though we know that they are dead in sin, and that faith is the work of the Spirit of God. Our faith enables us in God's name to command dead ones to live, and they do live. We bid unbelieving people believe in Jesus, and power goes with the Word, and God's elect do believe. It is by this word of faith which we preach that the voice of Jesus sounds out to humanity. The young man who could not rise, for he was dead, nevertheless did rise when Jesus bade him. Even so, when the Lord speaks by His servants, the Gospel command, "Believe and live," is obeyed and men and women live.

But the Savior, you observe, *spoke with His own authority*—"Young man, *I say unto thee*, Arise." Neither Elijah nor Elisha could thus have spoken, but He who spoke thus was very God of very God. Though veiled in human flesh and clothed in lowliness, He was that same God who said, "Let there be light," and there was light. If any of us are able by faith to say, "Young man, Arise," we can only say it in His name— we have no authority but what we derive from Him. Young man, young woman, the voice of Jesus can do what your mother cannot. How often has her sweet voice wooed you to come to Jesus, but wooed in vain! Oh, that the Lord Jesus would inwardly speak to you! Oh, that He would say, "Young man, Arise." I trust that while I am speaking the Lord is silently speaking in your hearts by His Holy Spirit. I feel sure that it is even so. If so, within you a gentle movement of the Spirit is inclining you to repent and yield your heart to Jesus. This shall be a blessed day to the spiritually dead young person, if now he accepts his Savior, and yields himself up to be renewed by grace. No, my poor friend, they shall not bury you! I know you have been very bad, and they may well despair of you, but while Jesus lives we cannot give you up.

The miracle was wrought straightway: for this young man, to the astonishment of all about him, sat up. His was a desperate case, but death was conquered for he sat up. He had been called back from the innermost dungeon of death, even from the grave's mouth, but he sat up when Jesus called him. It did not take a month, nor a week, nor an hour, no, not even five minutes. Jesus said, "Young man, Arise." "And he that was dead sat up, and began to speak." In an instant the Lord can save a sinner. Before the words I speak can have more than entered your ear, the divine flash which gives you eternal life can have penetrated your breast, and you shall be a new creature in Jesus Christ, beginning to live in newness of life; born this hour, no more to feel spiritually dead or to return to your old corruption. New life, new feeling, new love, new hopes, new company shall be yours because you have passed from death to life. Pray God that it may be so, for He will hear us.

This Will Produce Very Great Results

To give life to the dead is no little matter. The great result was manifest, first, in the young man. Would you like to see him as he was? Might I venture to draw back the sheet from his face? See there what death has done. He was a fine young man. To his mother's eye he was the image of manhood! What a pallor is on that face! How sunken are the eyes! You are feeling sad. I see you cannot bear the sight. Come, look into this grave, where corruption has gone further in its work. Cover him up! We cannot bear to look at the decaying body! But when

Jesus Christ has said, "Arise," what a change takes place! Now you may look at him. His blue eye has the light of heaven in it; his lips are coral red with life; his brow is fair and full of thought. Look at his healthy complexion, in which the rose and the lily sweetly contend for mastery. What a fresh look there is about him, as of the dew of the morning! He has been dead, but he lives and no trace of death is on him. While you are looking at him he begins to speak. Music for his mother's ear! What did he say? Why, that I cannot tell you. Speak yourself as a newly quickened one, and then I shall hear what you say. I know what I said. I think the first word I said when I was quickened was, "Hallelujah." Afterward, I went home to my mother and told her that the Lord had met with me. No words are given here. It does not quite matter what those words are, for any words proved him to be alive. If you know the Lord, I believe you will speak of heavenly things. I do not believe that our Lord Jesus has a dumb child in His house. They all speak to Him, and most of them speak of Him. The new birth reveals itself in confession of Christ and praise of Christ. I warrant you, that his mother when she heard him speak did not criticize what he said. She did not say, "That sentence is ungrammatical." She was too glad to hear him speak at all that she did not examine all the expressions which he used. Newly saved souls often talk in a way which later years and experience will not justify. You often hear it said of a revival meeting that there was a good deal of excitement, and certain young converts talked absurdly. That is very likely. But if genuine grace was in their souls, and they bore witness to the Lord Jesus, I for one would not criticize them very severely. Be glad if you can see any proof that they are born again, and mark well their future lives. To the young man himself a new life had begun—life born among the dead.

A new life also had begun in reference to *his mother.* What a great result for her was the raising of her dead son! Henceforth he would be doubly dear. Jesus helped him down from the bier and delivered him to his mother. We have not the words He used, but we are sure that He made the presentation most gracefully, giving back the son to the mother as one presents a choice gift. With a majestic delight which always goes with His condescending benevolence, He looked on that happy woman and His glance was brighter to her than the light of the morning, as He said to her, "Receive thy son." The thrill of her heart was such as she would never forget. Observe carefully that our Lord, when He puts the new life into young people, does not want to take them away with Him from the home where their first duty lies. Here and there one is called away to be an apostle or a missionary, but usually He wants them to go home to their friends and bless their parents and make their families happy and holy. He does not present the young man to the priest, but

He delivers him to his mother. Do not say, "I am converted, and therefore I cannot go to business anymore or try to support my mother by my trade." That would prove that you were not converted at all. You may go for a missionary in a year or two's time if you are fitted for it, but you must not make a dash at a matter for which you are not prepared. For the present go home to your mother and make your home happy, charm your father's heart, and be a blessing to your brothers and sisters and let them rejoice because "he was dead, and is alive again; he was lost, and is found."

What was the next result? Well, all the neighbors feared and glorified God. If yonder young woman who last night was at the music hall, and a few nights ago came home very nearly drunk—if that young woman is born again, all around her will wonder at it. If that young man who has got himself out of a situation by gambling, or some other wrong doing, is saved, we shall all feel that God is very near us. If that young man who has begun to associate with evil women and to fall into other evils is brought to be pure-minded and gracious, it will strike awe into those around him. She has led many others astray, and if the Lord now leads her back it will make a great hubbub, and people will inquire as to the reason of the change, and will see that there is a power in religion after all. Conversions are miracles which never cease. These prodigies of power in the moral world are quite as remarkable as prodigies in the material world. We want conversion so practical, so real, so divine that those who doubt will not be able to doubt because they see in them the hand of God.

Finally, note that it not only surprised the neighbors and impressed them, but the rumor of it went everywhere. Who can tell? If a convert is made this morning the result of that conversion may be felt for thousands of years, if the world stands so long; ay, it shall be felt when a thousand thousand years have passed away, even throughout eternity. Tremblingly have I dropped a smooth stone into the lake this morning. It has fallen from a feeble hand and from an earnest heart. Your tears have shown that the waters are stirred. I perceive the first circlet upon the surface. Other and wider circles will follow as the sermon is spoken of and read. When you go home and tell what God has done for your soul, there will be a wider ring; and if it should happen that the Lord should open the mouth of one of this morning's converts to preach His Word, then no one can tell how wide the circle will become. Ring upon ring will the word spread itself, until the shoreless ocean of eternity shall feel the influence of this morning's word. No, I am not dreaming. According to our faith so shall it be. Grace this day bestowed by the Lord upon one soul may affect the whole mass of humanity. God grant His blessing, even life forevermore. Pray much for a blessing. My dear friends, I beseech you, for Jesus Christ's sake, pray much for me. Amen.